Mindfulness in the

This book is an accessible companion for all early years practitioners to explore how mindfulness can be integrated into an early years learning environment. It presents topical theory and research, giving practical advice on using mindfulness as an everyday pedagogical tool to improve the emotional wellbeing of children, families and staff members.

Providing a step-by-step approach for adopting mindfulness practices, the book offers photocopiable resources, information on mindfulness techniques and opportunities for critical reflection to help create a 'mindful early years curriculum'. Chapters follow the four pillars of Calm, Acceptance, Relational Approach and Empathy, and include:

- The benefits of adopting a mindful approach in the early years

- The importance of staff wellbeing

- A template mindful curriculum for practitioners to adapt and use

- Case studies of effective mindful practices

- Resources, activities and techniques to create your own mindfulness toolkit

This delightful book will be a source of inspiration for early years practitioners, early years teachers and those who are interested in introducing and embedding mindfulness into early years practice.

Yasmin Mukadam is an author, teacher, further education lecturer and consultant in the field of early years. As an advisor for under 5s health and researcher in mindfulness, she works with early years settings and the health sector to promote children's mental health and wellbeing. She continues to teach early years courses and qualifications including neuroscience, emotional literacy, child development, yoga and mindfulness.

'*Mindfulness in the Early Years* will challenge practitioners thinking and provide positive change for both young children and those working in the early years sector. Yasmin Mukadam uses fresh innovative ways to demonstrate how we can best support children's mental health and well-being through mindfulness. This inspiring book also recognises current challenges teachers and practitioners face and provides invaluable strategies to overcome these. There could be no better time than present for this essential read, I highly recommend this book for all those who are studying or caring for young children within an Early Years setting.'

Claire Deadman, Nursery Manager

'This comprehensive guide provides invaluable insights and practical strategies for integrating mindfulness into the early years learning environment. With a strong foundation in research evidence and pedagogical approaches, Yasmin empowers educators to support children's mental health and well-being through reflective tasks, activities, and case studies. The book not only emphasises the importance of mindfulness for children but also highlights the significance of cultivating mindfulness in educators themselves. It is a must-have resource for early years degree students, practitioners, and teachers striving to create emotionally literate and mindful learning environments. I highly recommend this book to all early years professionals.'

Debra Corboy - Senior Lecturer, Morley College London

'It is refreshing, after working with children for over 30 years, to read a book that finally emphasises the impact an EYP/EYT can have on a child if their own mental health is not secure. The Pandemic left behind a huge MH Legacy, not just for the children, and this book can support the staff to acknowledge this, as well as offering practical support through personal mindfulness activities. This book is essential in supporting the children you care for, to understand the need for daily mindfulness, and to enable them to have a happy and healthy environment.'

Helen Sachania - External Quality Assurer (Health, Childcare and Education)

Mindfulness in the Early Years

Strategies and Approaches to Nurturing Young Minds

Yasmin Mukadam

Routledge
Taylor & Francis Group

LONDON AND NEW YORK

Designed cover image: © Getty Images

First edition published 2024
by Routledge
4 Park Square, Milton Park, Abingdon, Oxon, OX14 4RN

and by Routledge
605 Third Avenue, New York, NY 10158

Routledge is an imprint of the Taylor & Francis Group, an informa business

© 2024 Yasmin Mukadam

British Library Cataloguing-in-Publication Data
A catalogue record for this book is available from the British Library

ISBN: 978-0-367-14206-3 (hbk)
ISBN: 978-0-367-14208-7 (pbk)
ISBN: 978-0-429-03073-4 (ebk)

DOI: 10.4324/9780429030734

Typeset in Bembo Std
by KnowledgeWorks Global Ltd.

Contents

Acknowledgements

I would like to thank all my professional colleagues with whom I have worked with in further education, higher education and within the early years sector. You are all fantastic and amazing individuals!

I would like to give a special thanks to all my colleagues at Kingston University in the School of Education for inspiring and supporting me to pursue my research in the field of mindfulness and children's wellbeing.

A very special thank you to those who have contributed to this book. You are inspirational in the work that you do!

Lastly, I would especially like to thank my sons Sameen and Kamran for inspiring me to live each day with gratitude and kindness. You are my inspiration for all that I have achieved, and I am so proud of you both. A special thank you to my husband for your support and understanding throughout my career and endeavours.

My final thank you is to all the early years practitioners and teachers who continue to work tirelessly to support children's wellbeing and mental health. Let's continue to inspire children to flourish and grow into emotionally literate individuals.

Introduction

Welcome to Mindfulness in the Early Years! This book has been created as a companion for all early year's providers to explore how mindfulness can be integrated into an early year's learning environment and embedded as a pedagogical approach in supporting children's mental health and wellbeing.

The rationale for this book

This book is relevant for early years degree students, practitioners and teachers working in the education and health sector striving to support children's positive mental health and wellbeing. This practical handbook makes a relevant and helpful contribution in enabling practitioners and teachers to understand the context for mindfulness and how it can be introduced into their early years setting and curriculum.

The first part of the book encourages practitioners and teachers to explore both the theory and practice of supporting the positive mental health and wellbeing of children through mindfulness. They will gain the essential knowledge, skills and understanding of the research evidence and relevance of mindfulness in the field of early years. Throughout the book, reflective tasks, activities and case studies enable practitioners and teachers to develop a critical and reflective approach to their work, with opportunities to reflect on practice and apply strategies and models to create an effective emotionally literate learning environment.

The second part of the book provides one specific chapter that informs practitioners and teachers about the importance of mindfulness as a tool for enhancing their own wellbeing. Strategies and ideas are explored, with a range of mindfulness activities to consider and use. A range of specially designed toolkits enable practitioners and teachers to build their daily practice, learn about the value of mindfulness in their day-to-day role and apply it to daily life. A further chapter guides practitioners and teachers to introduce mindfulness into the curriculum and daily routine for children,

DOI: 10.4324/9780429030734-1

with a toolkit of mindfulness activities to enable you to create mindful opportunities for children.

Planning ideas and suggested resources are provided to support you to introduce mindful moments in a purposeful way, helping children to manage their thoughts and giving them the language, skills and confidence to regulate their emotions. All activities and techniques are closely linked to the Early Years Foundation Stage (EYFS) curriculum, with a step-by-step approach for practitioners and teachers to understand their role in planning a wellbeing curriculum whilst considering the important role of neuroscience in supporting and fostering children's self-regulation skills through mindfulness.

Finally, this book aims to empower early year's practitioners and teachers to support children to flourish and to fulfil their potential as 'every child deserves the best possible start in life' (DfE, 2021, p. 5). Definitions of mindfulness, pedagogy, wellbeing and mental health will be explored, and a range of approaches, techniques and tools will be discussed in order to enable a shift towards embedding mindfulness at the heart of your setting provision, practice and routines.

My hope is that you will be inspired by the content and build upon a toolkit of many effective mindfulness activities, play-based ideas and techniques that can be planned and implemented into your daily practice with children from birth to five years of age.

The case for mindfulness in the early years

You may have noticed how often children's mental health and wellbeing are mentioned in the news, daily planning conversations and within the education sector. A growing body of mindfulness research has now enabled sectors such as education to be more receptive to mindfulness practices in supporting children's wellbeing. Key influences impacting a mindfulness approach within early years are:

i. **Ofsted requirements**
   Alongside this, from 2015, the Ofsted framework required Ofsted inspectors to assess and report on pupils' mental health and wellbeing under the key judgment area of personal development, behaviour and welfare. This derived from government guidance introduced for schools called 'Promoting children and young people's emotional health and wellbeing'. This document clearly identified that 'a child's emotional health and wellbeing influences their cognitive development and learning, as well as their physical and social health and their mental wellbeing in adulthood' (2015, p. 4).

   The Ofsted Education Inspection Framework (2019, p. 11) published in May 2019 for implementation in September 2019 highlighted that:

   > Inspectors will make a judgement on the personal development of learners by evaluating the extent to which:

the curriculum and the provider's wider work support learners to develop their character – including their resilience, confidence and independence – and help them know how to keep physically and mentally healthy.

This emphasises the importance of settings to demonstrate their adoption to include wellbeing within the curriculum, thus increasing the interest to adopt approaches such as 'mindfulness practice' alongside other initiatives such as yoga as pivotal in enhancing children's resilience and helping them to keep mentally healthy.

ii. **Mental health and wellbeing**

The National Institute for Health and Care Excellence (NICE, 2016) advised schools to adopt a comprehensive 'whole school' approach to promoting the social and emotional wellbeing of children and young people in order to bring about sustaining health benefits. In addition, they provided mental health and wellbeing guidance to promote health and wellbeing of the under-fives, stating that social and emotional wellbeing provides the building blocks to healthy behaviours and educational attainment.

There is growing evidence of children's mental health problems in the early years, such as findings by a government NHS survey (2017) identifying that 1 in 18 pre-school children has a mental health disorder. Place2Be (2020) highlighted findings from a more recent NHS (2020) report, highlighting that the proportion of children experiencing mental health difficulties has increased over the past three years, from one in nine in 2017, to one in six as of July 2020, including depression, anxiety and conduct disorder.

iii. **Mindfulness research**

Katherine Weare's (2012) report, in association with the University of Exeter, summarises the scientific evidence base for the positive impact of mindfulness on a wide range of mental and physical health conditions, particularly social and emotional skills, wellbeing, learning and cognition. There is also 'good evidence from neuroscience and brain imaging that mindfulness meditation reliably and profoundly alters the structure and function of the brain to improve the quality of both thought and feeling' (Weare, 2012).

This growing body of evidence and government guidance has led to continued mindfulness interventions being introduced into settings and schools, setting a clear rationale to embed mindfulness within early years provision as a developing approach to enhance and support the mental health and wellbeing of the children.

iv. **Daily life stressors including the pandemic**

Today in this digital age, the way we live is much faster-paced than 30 years ago, with information at our fingertips and a busier and more fast-paced way of life. Children are faced with many challenges and stressors including busy daily routines, tendency towards a more indoor-based, sedentary lifestyle influenced by technology and social media. Other stressors include learning new skills, making friendships, transitions in the home and early years environment including bereavements, moving home, financial difficulties, ongoing assessments and exams, all of which affect wellbeing, feelings and emotions.

Alongside this, the coronavirus (COVID-19) pandemic is likely to have a long-term impact on children's mental health and wellbeing, according to a report by The Children's Society (2021). This report identified that the coronavirus pandemic has disrupted the life of every child with the closure of schools and many settings, and rising pressure on health services. Therefore, with interventions such as yoga, mindfulness and meditation, the need to support children's self-regulation has become an increased priority in early years to build these foundational skills and positively impact children's overall wellbeing and early brain development, known to have a 'pivotal impact on developmental outcomes including social and emotional wellbeing and academic functioning' (Kaunhoven and Dorjee, 2017). Five years on, a subsequent report by The Children's Society (2021) highlights that as the UK emerge from the coronavirus restrictions, although families and children coped to some extent with the pandemic restrictions, there is still work to do in terms of disruption to children's wellbeing and education.

v. Developing mindfulness practices in early years

The foundations for this book are built upon my interest and ability to raise awareness, understanding and strategies for implementing mindfulness into early years settings. This has been achieved whilst:

- Working in early years settings as a teacher, early years practitioner (EYP) and senior manager to plan and model mindfulness activities within the daily routine and curriculum.

- Teaching mindfulness at the college and university level.

- Consulting with a range of early years settings to improve the emotional curriculum and staff understanding of developing children's self-regulation skills.

- Carrying out my own research within the field of mindfulness, working with university colleagues and early years professionals within settings.

My intention is to enable you to develop an informed understanding of mindfulness in education and to provide you with a toolkit for creating a wellbeing curriculum within your setting with mindfulness at its core.

The ideas, activities and information within these chapters are intended to support you, the reader in reflecting upon your setting's provision and practice, identifying where the culture, curriculum and pedagogy can be adapted and improved upon to support the unique needs of every child and their wellbeing.

Aims of the book

This book is intended as a companion as well as a source of inspiration for EYPs, early years teachers (EYTs) and those who are interested in introducing and embedding mindfulness into early years practice.

The over-arching aim is to provide *a step-by-step approach* to adopt mindfulness practices within an existing early year's curriculum to create a 'mindful early year's curriculum'. The book intends to:

- Identify the benefits of adopting a mindful approach to your early year's pedagogy and practice and understand the importance of neuroscience and mindfulness research to support the case for mindfulness.

- Share resources, activities, case studies and provide insight into existing mindfulness programmes and influential mindfulness experts to inform your knowledge and future practice.

- Explain the importance of staff wellbeing and discuss strategies to support the mindfulness of early year's practitioners to develop and embed a wellbeing culture in the setting.

- Provide a template mindful curriculum as a guide for practitioners to adapt and use for their settings. This mindful curriculum guide will include a range of techniques, activities and ideas that are play-based and will enhance emotional resilience, self-regulation, social, emotional and mental health needs of children.

- Provide case studies of how effectively mindfulness can be introduced within early year's provision. These highlight the forward-thinking initiatives of EYPs in adopting mindfulness to support children's wellbeing and move towards a more coherent wellbeing-focused curriculum and setting culture.

- Strategies for embedding mindfulness within early years and looks to a future vision of a mindful curriculum that focuses 100% on the individual needs of children, with supportive adults who enable children to learn and develop in a calming and nurturing environment so that they fulfil their potential and lead happy and healthy lives.

Within each chapter of the book, you will find questions or activities to support your learning and understanding. Additionally, the book provides relevant case studies providing reflections from professionals working within early years environments. They identify the benefits of mindfulness and the positive impact on children's and staff's mental health and wellbeing.

Each chapter within the book will focus on an aspect of early years and how this can be adapted to embed and incorporate mindfulness at its heart. **Each chapter is interlinked by the four pillars of a mindful early year's curriculum, as illustrated below**.

Figure 0.1 **Four pillars of a mindful early years curriculum.**

These components represent an aspect of early years that can be reviewed and developed by the staff team when developing a mindfulness curriculum for their early year's provision.

The benefit of encompassing all four components is to fully embed a mindful approach to your daily routines and practice, which will enable you to develop a more relational approach to nurturing and supporting children's emotional wellbeing and overall learning and development. This will increase opportunities for children to self-regulate, develop their social and emotional skills, foster curiosity, confidence and provide opportunities for calm and supportive routines alongside the creative, curious and experiential play opportunities that provide the foundational skills for early childhood and later life.

The four pillars of a mindful early years curriculum are:

1. **C**alm

2. **A**cceptance

3. **R**elational approach

4. **E**mpathy

Figure 0.1 sets out four pillars which provide the building blocks to a mindful curriculum and are explained further within the book.

Scope of each chapter

Each chapter is outlined below and sets the framework for understanding the benefits to children and adults of developing a culture of mindfulness and the process for creating a curriculum, environment and pedagogy geared towards enhancing children's emotional wellbeing and mental health.

Chapter 1: Introducing mindfulness into early years

This chapter intends to explore the term mindfulness so that EYPs new or familiar with the term understand what it means when talking about 'being mindful' or 'developing a mindful practice in early years'. You will gain a better understanding and awareness of the background and the potential benefits of introducing mindfulness within an early year's environment and educational context. The chapter will explore definitions and aspects of mindfulness, wellbeing and mental health with awareness of the importance of early intervention to support increasing mental health problems on the rise in children and young people. Links to key influencers and the origins of mindfulness are outlined, with a look at some of the research evidence for introducing mindfulness within schools and early years practice. The chapter will make links to the importance of early intervention concluding with a case study providing insight into the impact of introducing mindfulness into practice.

Chapter 2: The mindful pedagogy

This chapter will identify how practitioners can create an early year's environment that embeds mindfulness at the heart of the daily curriculum. Definitions of pedagogy and mindfulness are explored as a first step towards creating a mindful pedagogy within your early year's provision. Strategies to develop a child-centred philosophy are discussed in creating an emotionally literate and supportive daily practice for children, where self-regulation is promoted through effective co-regulation. The chapter will provide insight into how research in the area of neuroscience is informing us about early brain development, the role of the limbic system, the area of the brain where our moods, actions, emotions and memories are controlled, and how thoughts and feelings can be supported by adults. A case study will provide insight into the impact of developing a wellbeing curriculum.

Chapter 3: Developing mindful environments in early years

This chapter introduces EYPs and EYTs to the importance of developing the indoor and outdoor environment so that children have the ability to bond with the natural world, experiencing a sense of freedom to venture beyond their know experiences with confidence and guidance from practitioners/teachers. A range of strategies will be introduced that can be adopted to enable a sense of calmness and self-expression during the daily routine, instilling moments for children and practitioners/teachers to experience present-moment awareness and build inner peace and quietness of the mind. The chapter will also focus on introducing areas of the environment where creative experiences are supported through play, movement, visualisations, games and yoga.

An effective audit tool for practitioners/teachers will be introduced to provide an effective mechanism to assess the current environment and its suitability in enhancing the emotional wellbeing of children. A case study will focus on developing a learning environment that is central to supporting wellbeing within practice.

Chapter 4: Mindfulness for staff wellbeing

This chapter introduces the benefits of mindfulness for staff in early years settings. It recognises the role of the adult in building resilience and a positive mental state within the work environment for themselves and with children. The chapter provides a range of mindfulness techniques and activities that can be practised, introduced and incorporated within daily life to support their mental health and wellbeing.

It goes onto explore some of the current issues impacting staff wellbeing and provides a range of models and strategies to manage change and manage challenging situations in the work setting. A case study will provide ideas and evidence-based outcomes of mindful techniques that work in supporting staff wellbeing.

Chapter 5: Mindfulness activities for children in early years

This chapter will provide an essential guide with a range of resources, activities and techniques for your early years setting that support children to be mindful, healthy and resilient. This practical guide will provide a bank of daily songs, rhymes, stories and physical activities to enhance children's self-expression and wellbeing across each age group: birth to 18 months, 18 months to 3 years and 3 to 5 years.

The chapter will enable practitioners and teachers to develop their own toolkit and create practices to support each child, embedding mindfulness as part of the daily routine to support transitions and provide a calming and balanced curriculum. Activities will be presented in a table for each age group within the prime and specific areas of learning and development. This practical chapter will share ideas of developing experiences that are underpinned to practices within an international context with links and examples from early year's settings and curricula in Spain, Norway, Italy and Sweden. The chapter will conclude with why practising mindfulness with children is important and how this can be done in a fun, practical and creative way and support children's ability to fulfil their potential in each area.

Chapter 6: The future of mindfulness in early years

This final chapter provides a perfect opportunity for EYPs and EYTs to review practices and introduce a mindful based curriculum to enable children to self-regulate and develop resilience within the early years. From the first lockdown when most early years settings closed, to the challenging period of re-opening and taking stock of the challenges that lay ahead, the resilience of the sector is acknowledged and the importance of supporting children's self-regulation, vital for their mental health and wellbeing. As settings adapted to social distancing measures, stringent health and safety procedures and policy changes, these circumstances ultimately put the early year's workforce under increased levels of stress, anxiety and fear and concern for the future health and wellbeing of children and staff. The future vision for mindfulness in early years is also discussed in this final chapter, and a range of resources for further information provides a starting point to build knowledge and give the sector and workforce the recognition to remain resilient and exceed expectations in meeting the care and education needs of families in England.

References

Department for Education (DfE) (2021) *Statutory Framework for the Early Years Foundation Stage: Setting the Standards for Learning, Development and Care for Children from Birth to Five*. Accessed on 15 May 2022 at https://assets.publishing.service.gov.uk/government/uploads/system/uploads/attachment_data/file/974907/EYFS_framework_-_March_2021.pdf

Kaunhoven, R. J. and Dorjee, D. (2017) 'How Does Mindfulness Modulate Self-Regulation in Pre-Adolescent Children? An Integrative Neurocognitive Review', *Journal: Neuroscience and Bio-Behavioural Reviews Journal*, 74(2017), pp. 163–184.

National Health Service (NHS) (2017) *Mental Health of Children and Young People*, 2017. Accessed on 15 November 2022 at https://digital.nhs.uk/data-and-information/publications/statistical/mental-health-of-children-and-young-people-in-england/2017/2017

National Institute for Care and Health Excellence (NICE) (2016) *Early Years: Promoting Health and Wellbeing in Under 5s*. Accessed on 18 June 2023 at https://www.nice.org.uk/guidance/qs128/resources

Office for Standards in Education (Ofsted) (2019) The education inspection framework. Accessed on 20 May 2022 at https://www.gov.uk/government/publications/education-inspection-framework/education_inspection-framework

Place2be (2020) *New Report from NHS Digital shows sharp increase in children experiencing mental health difficulties*. Accessed on 10 February 2021 at https://www.place2be.org.uk/about-us/news-and-blogs/2020/october/new-report-from-nhs-digital-shows-sharp-increase-in-children-experiencing-mental-health-difficulties/

The Children's Society (2021) *The Good Childhood Report 2021*. Accessed on 18 August 2021 at https://www.childrenssociety.org.uk/sites/default/files/2021-08/GCR_2021_Summary_0.pdf

Weare, K. (2012) *Evidence for the Impact of Mindfulness on Children and Young People (The Mindfulness in Schools Project Report)*. Accessed on 24 September 2021 at https://mindfulnessinschools.org/wp-content/uploads/2013/02/MiSP-Research-Summary-2012.pdf

Introducing mindfulness into early years

Introduction

This chapter introduces the importance of mindfulness within the early years' environment to early years practitioners (EYPs), early years teachers (EYTs) and other professionals.

'In recent years, there has been an increase in awareness, understanding and scientific research into the impact of mindfulness on our mental health' (Currid, 2020). It seems that mindfulness today is no longer a buzzword and is considered by health and education professionals as a technique to support mental health and wellbeing. Wedge (2018) suggests that 'because mindfulness promotes skills that are controlled in the prefrontal cortex of the brain, like the ability to focus and concentrate, it is especially useful for children'.

The term has continued to grow in recognition as a technique that can be adopted within educational settings, with Professor Mark Williams, former director of the Oxford Mindfulness Centre, succinctly identifying mindfulness as knowing directly what is going on inside and outside ourselves, moment by moment (NHS, 2021).

Virtually all early years professionals understand the importance of the first five years of children's lives, with rapid growth and brain development laying the foundations of health, wellbeing and happiness. It is now more important than ever before that education professionals consider the best approaches for future early years provision, in

DOI: 10.4324/9780429030734-2

terms of children's health, safety and wellbeing. Following the worldwide coronavirus disease 2019 (Covid-19) pandemic since 2020, there has been a big shift in working practices, particularly within early years settings. Planned policy changes, procedures and health and safety practices are reviewed to ensure children grow and flourish in a healthy and safe environment. This is a fundamental priority to ensure low risk and harm from Covid-19 now and in the future. In addition to risk assessments and safe working practices, children's mental health is now more vital to daily planning and routines. This chapter starts to unpick how a wellbeing focused curriculum is a priority for children's wellbeing, with mindfulness interventions to guide their care, learning and development and to protect the health and wellbeing of all practitioners too.

What is mindfulness?

Mindfulness is a quality that every human being already possesses. It is the ability to train our mind to be fully present in the moment, without it wandering around from the past into the future.

At a simplistic level, mindfulness is about being present with whatever experiences and feelings we hold right now; it is about inviting a different relationship to our thoughts, emotions and feelings; one of kindness, awareness and acceptance.

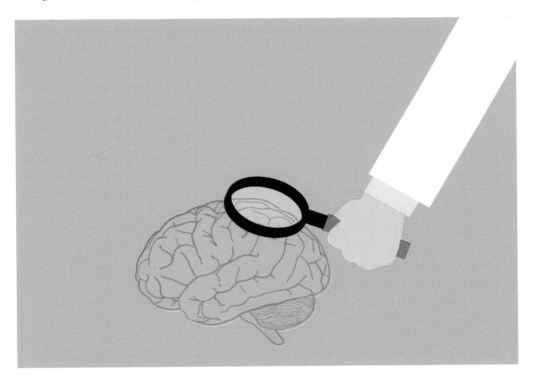

Figure 1.1   **Brain and magnifying glass.**

Dr. Jon Kabat-Zinn coined the term mindfulness with a definition well regarded today in scholarly research throughout the world. He defines mindfulness as 'paying attention in a particular way on purpose, in the present moment, and non-judgmentally' (Kabat-Zinn, 2003, p. 145).

Kabat-Zinn recognises that mindfulness is one of the hardest things in the world for humans to tap into consistently; however, he suggests that the invitation of being mindful is always the same: 'stop for a moment and drop into wakefulness' holding the moment in awareness as it is. He adds that,

> if we miss this moment because we are distracted or caught up in thinking, or in our emotions or busyness of what always seems to need getting done, there is always the next moment to stop and drop into wakefulness – a new moment.
>
> (Wbur, 2018)

This is agreed by Weare (2013), who suggests that mindfulness is essentially about paying attention to the here and now and living in the present moment.

In terms of application, Jones (2011) defines mindfulness as a series of simple meditation style exercises that 'increase awareness of the contents of our minds, and provide ways to respond to our thoughts and feelings "skilfully" such that they are less likely to lead to emotional distress of harmful behaviours'.

This is supported by Erwin and Robinson (2015, p. 1) who identify that mindfulness is receiving more attention than ever before, with the Good Child Report (The Children's Society, 2016, p. 3) backing this up by suggesting that 'at a time when children's mental health is of increasing concern' the links between wellbeing and mental health issues are now more recognised within the education field.

Mindfulness is more important than ever before, with Professor Williams asserting that mindfulness allows us to become more aware of the stream of thoughts and feelings that we experience, allowing us to then stand back from those thoughts and start to observe patterns (NHS, 2021), further adding how we are then able to gradually train ourselves to notice when our thoughts are taking over and realise that 'thoughts are simply mental events that do not have to control us'.

My research with teachers and children in early years has prompted me to offer a definition of mindfulness that is considerate of both children and adults: 'consciously pausing and tuning into our physical and mental state, acknowledging thought patterns, inner dialogue and surroundings without judgment'.

Bishop et al. (2004) provide a clear 'operational definition'. Their understanding of mindfulness is two-fold:

> The first component involves the self-regulation of attention so that it is maintained on immediate experience, thereby allowing for increased recognition of mental

events in the present moment. The second component involves adopting a particular orientation toward one's experiences in the present moment, an orientation that is characterized by curiosity, openness, and acceptance.

Daily mindfulness in practice

We live in a sensory world and although we tend not to notice, we are using our senses in every moment. The experience of our senses overlapping, blending and cross-pollinating as we make sense of the world, day to day and moment to moment relates to an experience identified by Wbur (2018) as synaesthesia. To put this into context, try this activity.

Activity

For a few moments, imagine walking through the park, being immersed in nature, woodlands, amongst trees, greenery, the beauty of the natural world all around you.

Through our senses we immediately begin to notice feelings of inner calm, peace and stillness around us. This is experienced through all our senses and tends to bring us into present moment awareness, without the distractions of our somewhat busy lives that can limit our opportunities from 'being' to 'doing' mode.

This sensory experience tends to bring us into present moment awareness

---

The good news is that mindfulness moments can be practised and built into our daily lives using simple tools and techniques that ultimately support our mental health and wellbeing. Research supporting the benefits of mindfulness and how it affects and changes brain structure and function is explained briefly in this chapter and sections throughout the book.

Mindfulness activity: The five senses exercise

- This is a simple activity that can be done with adults and children any time in the day, taking only a few minutes and in any situation.

- All that is needed is for the child or adult to notice and feel through each of the five senses.

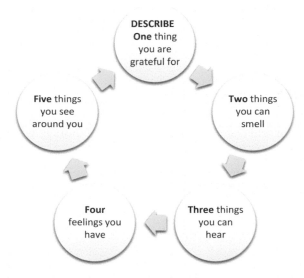

Figure 1.2 **The five senses activity cycle.**

Mindfulness can be taught or modelled as a core skill to support a child or adult to gain awareness of their own thoughts and feelings. This supports self-regulation, a vital skill to support emotion regulation.

Self-regulation: What is it and why is it important for children's learning and wellbeing?

As early years professionals, we are seeing a generation of children with high levels of stress and mental health disorders. There are many hidden stressors that children are struggling with: physiological as well as social and emotional. 'The proportion of children experiencing a probable mental health disorder has increased in the past three years, from one in nine in 2017 to one in six in July 2020' (NHS Digital, 2020). We know that children's emotional wellbeing is just as important as their physical health. Fostering self-regulation skills in children is now a more prominent feature of the revised Development Matters Framework (Department for Education (DfE), 2020). Dr Julian Grenier, who led on the most changes to the guidance, identifies the importance of self-regulation skills for children's early learning, and also their lifelong mental health and wellbeing (2021).

Dr. Stuart Shanker (2021), a prolific researcher in self-regulation, founded The MEHRIT Centre and developed a significant body of significant research, with a definition suggesting that self-regulation is, a child's ability to deal with stressors effectively and efficiently, and then return to a baseline of being calmly focused and alert. His research identifies the role of self-regulation in mental and physical wellbeing and academic achievement, alongside the benefits that positive stress plays in children's development and learning, and the worrying effects of excessive negative stress.

EYPs and EYTs work daily to support the healthy holistic development of children. It is fundamental to understand that you need to pay close attention to the child's self-regulation and to help each child to recognise stressors that may occur and help to reduce these stressors and bring them back to a calm and focused state of mind, using Shanker's five-step approach that gives them the skills to manage their emotions and improve their ability to self-regulate. Conkbayir (2020) adds that self-regulation is 'one's ability to manage one's own emotional responses and consequent behaviour and knowing how to control those big, overwhelming feelings such as anger or fear, in order to get on with the serious business of play, building relationships and learning. In short, being able to self-regulate is how we manage stress'.

Shanker (2021) suggests that the more stressors a child is dealing with, the harder it becomes to remain calmly focused and alert. Something crucial to be aware of is that a child's negative behaviour is not some sort of 'innate' character flaw, but a chronic state of being over-aroused that is draining his capacity to deal with new stressors.

Children's capacity for self-regulation is developing in the early years, and Shanker identifies five accessible steps that parents, professionals and caregivers can apply to address self-regulation skills in children to support their wellbeing.

Shanker's five steps of self-regulation are:

1. Read the signs of stress and reframe the behaviour (learn the difference between misbehaviour and stress behaviour).

2. Recognise the stressors.

3. Reduce the stress.

4. Reflect: enhance stress awareness.

5. Respond: help the child learn to respond to stressors and return to calm (restore energy).

According to Shanker (2017), these practices have proven very successful in helping parents and teachers nurture happier and healthier children. They apply to individuals, groups of children and to caregivers themselves.

We know that while most children grow up emotionally healthy and happy, however, they are experiencing more mental health issues nowadays than 30 years ago, possibly due to the way in which we live our lives in a busy and fast paced manner.

A National Trust report (Moss, 2012) supports this by identifying a modern phenomenon when focusing on the lives of children in the UK, known as 'Nature Deficit Disorder' that Moss links to poverty and technology. The report highlights the lack of children's engagement with nature and connection to the natural world. It also highlights concern that if the trend towards a sedentary, indoor childhood continues, statistics and results of studies and surveys confirm 'the dramatic and worrying consequences linked to three specific categories: physical health problems including obesity, mental health problems and children's growing inability to assess risks to themselves and others' (Moss, 2012, p. 3). This demonstrates the importance of addressing mental wellbeing and implementing effective interventions such as mindfulness at a young age to foster self-regulation skills.

What is wellbeing?

The term 'wellbeing' is widely used within health and education settings. It is important, therefore, to establish a clear understanding at the outset, with an awareness that beliefs and values regarding this term can vary between individuals, settings, sectors and countries.

Statham and Chase (2010, p. 12) define the term wellbeing as 'a dynamic state that is enhanced when people can fulfil their personal and social goals'. They emphasise that childhood wellbeing is not only complex but multi-dimensional, and should include dimensions of physical, social and emotional wellbeing.

Children's wellbeing is a fundamental component in enabling every baby, toddler and pre-schooler to achieve their potential within the early years of their life. This notion is supported with a definition that 'wellbeing represents an ultimate and universal goal of human existence' (New Economics Foundation (NEF), 2014).

Supporting young children's emotional wellbeing is at the core of the early years foundation stage (EYFS) and is certainly a significant area that educational professionals need to be familiar with. It is important in terms of supporting self-regulation as a foundational skill required by each child to manage stressors in their lives and develop

Figure 1.3 **Children looking into the river.**

resilience for later life. By applying a more relational approach between practitioner and child to support emotional health, adults play a key role in scaffolding children's emotional wellbeing and overall holistic development. This is supported by the government's definition of wellbeing as 'a positive physical, social and emotional state' (Mental Health Foundation, 2016).

Ferre Laevers is infamously known to have developed the scales of wellbeing and involvement, specifically for EYPs to ensure that they are providing the right environment both emotionally and physically for learning to take place. Laevers wellbeing and involvement scales provide a base line for identifying children's emotional wellbeing with the intention that practitioners can then plan interventions to support and strengthen children's wellbeing and help them to understand their emotions and feelings (Laevers, 2005, p. 4).

What is mental health?

Good mental health continues to be a key agenda topic for the UK Government with a report by the Department of Health (2012) highlighting that 'mental health problems affect one in four of us at some time in our lives'. The cost of this to society is on average £105 billion every year. The Mental Health Foundation's handbook (Mental Health Foundation, 2016) informs us that one in four people in the UK will experience a mental health problem in any given year, and in the UK, mental health problems are responsible for the largest burden of disease at 28%. This highlights government objectives towards promoting good mental health for people of all ages.

This further emphasises the importance of the role of EYPs, EYTs and all professionals supporting children's mental health and wellbeing, with statistics highlighting that 'at present, one in ten children and young people suffer from mental health problems ... positive mental health enables children to develop their resilience and grow into well rounded adults' (MAPPG, 2015).

Figure 1.4 **Baby sleeping.**

Figure 1.5 **Woman standing with arms out to the side.**

One definition of the term mental health shows the interrelation that mindfulness has with other areas of health and wellbeing.

> Mental health is a state of wellbeing in which every individual realises his or her own potential, can cope with the normal stresses of life, can work productively and fruitfully, and are able to make a contribution to her or his community.
>
> (World Health Organization (WHO), 2014)

In order to understand why mindfulness is receiving so much attention, we only need to look as far as the National Health Service with the guidance and support being offered for an increasing number of people diagnosed with physical and mental health disorders. 'For people with both physical and mental health problems, recovery from each is delayed and the effect of poor mental health on physical illnesses is estimated to cost the NHS at least 8 billion a year' (Naylor et al., 2012, p. 12).

Therefore, reducing stress is a good starting point for improving health outcomes. Mindfulness offers an integrated mind-body approach that gives equal value to both entities (MAPPG, 2015, p. 20). There are many different advantages to re-shaping lifestyles to include mindfulness, ranging from improved wellbeing to greater resilience, making it a popular and cheaper prevention strategy against stress and to improved health outcomes.

Sowing the seeds of a mindful curriculum

Developing a curriculum with mindfulness at its core can take time and is supported with the strategies and step-by-step approach shared in this book. A good way to get started is to introduce some basic mindfulness techniques for children. From this you can assess the positive impact almost immediately! However, like any skill, mindfulness takes practice, so rather than worry about creating a mindful curriculum straight away, the aim is to start encompassing the four pillars in some quick mindful activities. Here are eight easy mindful exercises for you to try for yourself in your own life and then with children in your early years setting.

This is how the activities in Table 1.1 can be implemented, to embody the four pillars of a mindful curriculum:

1. **Calm** – Focus the children or self on being in the present moment, having awareness of what is happening right here right now; noticing sounds, activating the senses to feel and express emotions from the activities.

Table 1.1 Mindfulness Activities for Children and Adults in Early Years

Simple mindfulness activities for children and adults			
Mindful walk through the garden/park	Mindful eating at mealtimes	Belly breathing with favourite toy on belly	Yoga poses that focus on body movements
Talking about feelings and emotions	Glitter jar to support settling of emotions	Blowing bubbles and noticing breathing out	Body scan – mindful listening

2. **A**cceptance – Support children to co-regulate and accept how they are feeling in that moment; allow them to express themselves verbally, modelling stillness and noticing the breathe going in and out of the body.

3. **R**elational approach – Listen and observe without judgment, building a trusting relationship; if challenging behaviour is observed, focus on the inner emotions being felt by the child or self and acknowledge as the emotional brain starts to recognise and find ways to calm down.

4. **E**mpathy – Identify with the feelings and support the child or self to come back to a calm state if they are overwhelmed or showing negative behaviour; positive body language towards others' needs.

Remember to make time for each mindful activity, practising the art of mindfulness daily!

The origins of mindfulness

Mindfulness practices have become increasingly popular in the last decade. But where did mindfulness come from, and how have so many people in the west become very interested in it?

This is not a straightforward question to answer. However, one way to address this is to trace the origins of mindfulness from Eastern traditions to the secular presence that it holds within Western society with well-known practices such as yoga, breathwork and meditation.

People have been practising mindfulness for thousands of years in the East, either on their own or as part of a larger group. Mindfulness originated in Buddhist tradition as a practice to bring compassion and awareness to our thoughts, to strengthen the mind and to be fully present in our daily lives.

The term itself derives from the Buddhist word 'sati' and the Sanskrit term 'smrti' meaning 'to recollect' or 'to bear in mind'. Originally, it was confined to Buddhist monasteries of Southeast Asia some 2500 years ago. Today, however, mindfulness is used in the west in various traditions such as yoga and meditation, and within training and programmes to support stress reduction and mental health. The traditions of this practice have been applied to what we know as mindfulness today, that is, 'a daily relevance for calmness, insight and profound transformation of the mind' (Titmuss, 2014, p. 7).

It is important to note that 'some commentators argue that the history of mindfulness should not be reduced to Buddhism and Hinduism, as it also has roots in Judaism, Christianity and Islam (Trousselard et al., 2014). Many Western practitioners and teachers of mindfulness such as Jon Kabat-Zinn learned about mindfulness through the Hindu and Buddhist traditions, as well as practices in countries such as India, Japan and Tibet.

In 1979, John Kabat-Zinn introduced chronically ill patients who were not responding well to traditional treatments to participate in his newly formed eight-week stress reduction programme, now known as mindfulness-based stress reduction (MBSR). Since then, there has been substantial research demonstrated about how mindfulness–based interventions improve mental and physical health comparable to other psychological interventions. The many mindfulness teachers who advocate and encourage mindfulness believe it is an inherent human capability that belongs to us all (Boyce, 2018).

Mindfulness practices have become increasingly popular within education since the last decade in the UK. With the success of Kabat-Zinn's MBSR programme in healthcare settings, sparked what is now called 'The Mindfulness Movement', with the spread of MBSR and other mindfulness practices into areas including primary schools, prisons, sports, finance and even the British parliament (Fossas, 2015). Time magazine identified this era as the 'Mindful Revolution', suggesting that we are in the midst of a popular obsession with mindfulness as the secret to health and happiness alongside a growing body of evidence suggesting its benefits (Pickert, 2014).

Fast forward to today, we remain in a time when no one seems to have *enough* time in our day as technology and devices have made it easy for us to distract our attention from being in the here and now. On the positive side, this allows us in many places at once – but at the cost of being unable to fully inhabit the place where we actually want to be, in the present moment.

Activity

What is your definition of mindfulness?

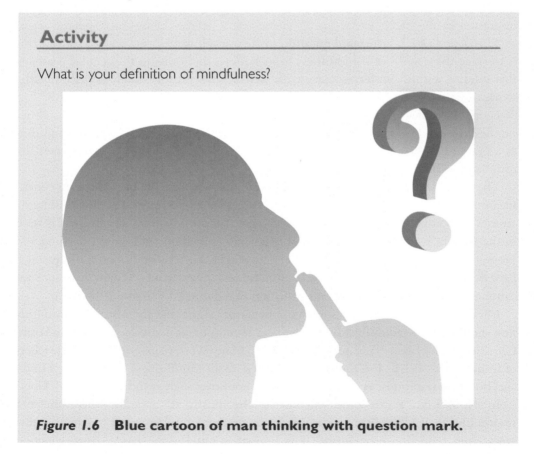

Figure 1.6 **Blue cartoon of man thinking with question mark.**

Reflect upon what you have understood about mindfulness so far, and write your current understanding of mindfulness here:

....

....

....

Next, reflect on where your perception of mindfulness has come from. It may be from your own self-practice, reading or your own research.

....

....

This is a simplistic definition that can be used when explaining mindfulness to a colleague, parent or other professional – 'mindfulness is pressing pause in our day to stop and notice our thoughts, feelings and emotions in the present moment'.

The good news is that mindfulness can be easily integrated into daily life, making it more appealing to create a curriculum with mindfulness embedded at its core. Mindfulness activities can be accessible for children within their daily routine through fun and creative ways, as we will discover in this book.

Identify two ways that you think mindfulness could be applied into your early year's curriculum for children?

1. ....

2. ....

Key influencers in the field of mindfulness

1. **Dr. Jon Kabat-Zinn:** A biologist who developed an MBSR at a Stress Reduction Clinic in Massachusetts in 1979. When working towards a PhD in molecular biology, he discovered meditation and Buddhist philosophy. This marked the beginning of his journey into sharing the impact of mindfulness in reducing stress and improving health.

He developed a Centre for Mindfulness, wrote several books and shared his work through mindfulness retreats and research. His work has gained a strong following particularly the MBSR programme, which is used today in the corporate world, in the health and education sectors and by UK government ministers as a way to reduce stress. The eight-week programme combines mediation exercises and yoga techniques to help individuals address symptoms including chronic pain and stress. Kabat-Zinn is well known for having researched the benefits of mindfulness, and his work attempts to integrate the body and mind to heal physical health symptoms as well as psychological stress. This is illustrated in his book 'Full Catastrophe Living: Using the Wisdom of your Body and Mind to Face Stress (Kabat-Zinn, 1990). He describes mindfulness as 'moment-to-moment, non-judgmental awareness on the physical body, the immune system and stress' (1990).

2. **William Kuyken:** Principal Investigator and Director at the University of Oxford Mindfulness Research Centre. He gained a Doctorate in Clinical Psychology and developed a training programme in mindfulness-based cognitive therapy (MBCT) in the 1990s. He has also contributed to MBSR workshops, retreats, clinical psychology research and programmes when working at the University of Exeter from 1999 to 2014.

   Kuyken's work focuses on evidence-based approaches to depression, and his research examines how mindfulness and mindfulness-based programmes can prevent depression and improve human potential. There have been several studies that have arisen from his work, suggesting MBCT as an alternative to antidepressants.

   His most recent work in 2018 looked into mindfulness-based interventions and their effectiveness into improving the behavioural, cognitive and mental health outcomes of children and adolescents. He has devised mindfulness-based approaches for adults and children with the aim to assess efficacy of a schools-based universal mindfulness intervention to enhance mental health and wellbeing.

There are other advocates who continue to inform us about the importance of mindfulness for children and adults, including:

■ Dr. Dan Siegel

■ Katherine Weare

■ Dr. Rick Hanson

■ Daniel Goleman

■ Richard Davidson

Activity

Read the definition of mindfulness and reflect on what parts of this definition you find most interesting and relevant to early years practice?

Mindfulness is the basic human ability to be fully present, aware of where we are and what we're doing, and not overly reactive or overwhelmed by what's going on around us.

....

....

....

....

....

Mindfulness in education research

The landscape for children's mental health and wellbeing

There is a growing body of research available to early years professionals showing how mindfulness helps to reduce children's anxiety and stress, improve memory and promote self-regulation and empathy (Mineo, 2018).

Mindfulness is receiving more recognition in the public arena than ever before, with a growing body of scientific research in many countries, including the UK. From their research, Erwin and Robinson (2015) remind us how mindfulness approaches are being introduced and perceived as beneficial to children during their early and primary school years, with evidence that positive mental health enables children to develop resilience and grow into well-rounded adults (Mind, 2015).

Katherine Weare, a leading figure in children's mindfulness research, conducted a study in 2013 to review the evidence for mindfulness and the policy context within the UK. Her findings highlighted a number of studies suggesting that 'When well taught and when practiced regularly mindfulness has been shown to be capable of improving mental health and wellbeing, mood, self-esteem, self-regulation, positive behaviour and academic learning' (Weare, 2013).

In her study, Sara Lazar (neuroscientist at Harvard Medical School) was the first to identify that mindfulness mediation can change regions within the brain linked to memory, the sense of self and regulation of emotions (Mineo, 2018).

The origins of mindfulness training programmes

Traditionally, mindfulness has been associated with adults and came to the attention of a wider audience in the UK when members of the UK Parliament promoted the benefits of mindfulness to mental health (MAPPG, 2015).

Today, a range of mindfulness training programmes, therapies, exercises and techniques have been adopted into Western society, arising from what is now one of the most widely recognised and predominant mindfulness-based programmes known.

In the late 1970s, Dr. Jon Kabat-Zinn developed an MBSR programme aimed to lower stress and enhance the wellbeing of patients suffering from anxiety and stress (Erwin et al., 2015). This infamous eight-week MBSR programme is today supported by many studies worldwide, alongside another MBCT programme, developed by Segal, Williams and Teasdale.

Mindfulness programmes today are known to help alleviate stress, anxiety, depression and chronic pain, combining mediation techniques, with cognitive behavioural skills and mindful movement relevant for everyday living.

From the original MBSR programmes, a range of mindfulness programmes have been developed for adults and children during the last two decades, including:

■ The Mind Up programme

■ Mindfulness in Schools Project

■ Mind Be Curriculum

Each programme recognises the growing need for supporting the education sector, supported by a range of studies identifying the value of mindfulness for children.

It is evident that much of the research on mindfulness and education still tends to be focused on older children, yet we know that the early years are a crucial time when foundations of learning are developed.

Mindfulness research supporting children's health and wellbeing

Today, a range of government reports and surveys highlight the importance of supporting the mental health and wellbeing in children and young people, most importantly a survey conducted by the NHS in England in 1999, 2004, 2017 and most recently 2020, the 'Mental Health of Children and Young People Survey' (NHS

Digital, 2020). The first two surveys provide comparable data for 5–15-year-olds, and for the first time, the (NHS, 2017) survey summarised findings of *mental health disorders in 2- to 4-year-old children*, summarised in Chapter 2. *The link providing further information relating to these surveys can be found in the reference list at the end of the chapter.*

This ongoing work by the government builds upon the work of UNICEF in 2007, in their report on child wellbeing, where the UK was ranked in the lowest quartile among 29 countries relating to six different aspects of wellbeing (UNICEF, 2007). This suggests that even as a relatively advanced nation, children's wellbeing and mental health remains an area of concern as more recently the 'Mental Health of Children and Young People Report' (2020) is the first in a series by the government (NHS) to explore the mental health of children and young people during the Covid-19 pandemic in July 2020. *The link that shares the report and findings can be found in the reference list at the end of the chapter.*

Research by the WHO shows the interrelation between mental health and interventions such as mindfulness, emphasising that mental health is a state of well-being in which every individual recognises his or her own potential and can cope with the normal stresses of life. The World Mental Health Report highlights that mental health is a vital element of individual and collective wellbeing (WHO, 2022).

With this in mind, mindfulness practices are increasingly being used with school-aged children and in early years settings. Research studies indicate that self-regulation skills in early childhood education can make a significant contribution to school readiness and long-term academic success (Dinehart and Willis, 2013). The study discusses the development of self-regulation skills specifically in relation to increased concentration, attention and awareness of social–emotional behaviours in children. Although research studies on mindfulness with children are still relatively new, the body of evidence continues to grow.

A pilot study by Nadler et al. (2017) identified that relatively little is known about the effects of mindfulness with children, particularly when briefer practices are used, and when children are young. However, this same pilot study reported that in two samples, where children aged 7–9 were assigned to a brief 10-minute mindfulness practice, they completed age appropriate self-report measures showing an increase in the domain of calmness. Burke (2009) identifies that mindfulness-based interventions aim to teach mindfulness skills to promote psychological health and well-being.

Table 1.2 provides a list of relevant studies that can be accessed, showing the potential benefits of mindfulness for children in early year's education.

Education policy

There has been a rise in interest within education policy in recent years in supporting children's emotional and mental health rather than focusing on children's physical growth and wellbeing.

Table 1.2 **Mindfulness Research Studies**

Author	Purpose of research article	Type of mindfulness practice
Flook et al. (2015) Region: USA	Study investigating the effects of a mindfulness programme to investigate prosocial behaviour and self-regulatory skills in preschool children.	12-week mindfulness curriculum
Region: India	Study examining how mindfulness practices build community with amongst a diverse population of children age 2–5 years.	Meditation and yoga
Region: Kuala Lumpar	Case study exploring potential effects of mindfulness practices on learning and educational experiences in early childhood.	Mindfulness approach
Cvitković (2021)	This study examines the possibilities of introducing yoga as part of the school curriculum for children.	
Region: South Korea	Article exploring mindful practices as ways to support children as they grow in body, mind and spirit, as a way to help them be happy.	Meditation, movement and relaxation
Region: USA	Study examining the effects of yoga in improving time on task for children exhibiting attention problems.	Yoga, relaxation and deep breathing
Capel (2012) Region: Malaysia	Study examining how mindful classroom practices affect the quality of learning and children's experiences in an early childhood educational setting.	Mindfulness approaches
Weare (2013) Region: UK	Review sharing the evidence of the impact of mindfulness for children and young people	Mindfulness approaches

The Allen Report (2011) highlighted children's social and emotional development as a 'bedrock' in supporting children's physical and mental health. It also identified that early intervention was imperative for the foundations of children's social and emotional development to 'help to keep them happy, healthy and achieving throughout their lives and, above all, equip them to raise children of their own, who will also enjoy higher levels of wellbeing' (Allen, 2001, p. 9, cited in Mukadam and Sutherland, 2018).

This key report informed Dame Clare Tickell's Review (2011) that led towards revisions to the EYFS (2012), with further revisions in 2014, 2017 and 2020, with further revisions in 2021 as identified by the Early Years Alliance (2021), stating that 'The Department for Education is to change the EYFS in 2021 with the government saying that the changes will 'improve outcomes for all children … and reduce teacher workload'. We know that once again, all changes will impact on daily practices, policies and paperwork, however, with a resilient workforce, the focus to nurture children's emotional wellbeing will continue to play a significant role.

The role of UNICEF and the All-Party Parliamentary Group (APPG)

UNICEF began making comparisons on child poverty within rich nations, leading to international league tables on child poverty, presented on Report Cards providing comprehensive estimates of child poverty across the industrialised world (UNICEF, 2000).

This led to ongoing reports on child wellbeing, in particular UNICEF's Report Cards 7 and 11 (UNICEF, 2013) measured child wellbeing as a dimension. The scores from Report Card 11 highlighted that wellbeing in the United Kingdom was ranked at 16th out of 29 OECD members of developed countries co-operating in this report.

Public interest to improve wellbeing and mental health within education arose following a one year long inquiry by the APPG. This group was formed in 2009 and after a break reconstituted in 2018. The group was commissioned by the government to research evidence of the benefits of mindfulness in the workplace and other settings such as healthcare, education and the criminal justice system.

The Wellbeing Economics report (NEF, 2014) clearly identified that the UK has become a leader in measuring wellbeing, yet wellbeing is not yet being widely used to inform policy with regards to improving child development and wellbeing, core to the principles of the EYFS framework.

The report set out clearly within four key policy areas how wellbeing evidence can be translated into policy in order to build a high wellbeing recovery within health and education. A key recommendation in the report was to introduce mindfulness into the basic training of teachers within the policy area building personal resources: mindfulness in health and education.

> Mindfulness has significant potential to improve wellbeing and save public money. A first key step for unlocking this potential is to train professionals such as teachers in mindfulness.
>
> (NEF, 2014, p. 32)

The Wellbeing Economics report (NEF, 2014) also identified that 'Mindfulness has significant potential to improve wellbeing and save public money'. Since then, the role of mindfulness in education continues to develop, indicating the positive impact it can have on wellbeing. Following this, the MAPGG (2015) published once again how mindfulness was on the government agenda. This report introduced mindfulness as an approach to reduce the mental health crisis that is increasing in the UK. The report sought to introduce mindfulness interventions within the areas of education and health, identifying an emerging body of evidence that suggests both parents and children can benefit from the practice of mindfulness (MAPPG, 2015).

Attachment theory and mindfulness

When children have a secure attachment with their parent or carer, it is an important protective factor for their mental health, while insecure attachments can be a risk factor for the development of emotional and behaviour problems. Insecure attachments develop if early interactions between a child and their caregiver are negative, inconsistent, inappropriate, neglectful or abusive (Mentally Healthy Schools, 2021). Nurturing and being responsive to children's emotional needs supports both positive relationships and those important early bonds between the infant and their primary caregiver.

John Bowlby's attachment theory provides the evidence-based underpinning that highlights the importance of this 'lasting psychological connectedness between human beings' (Cherry, 2019). The impact of this early relationship is central to the EYFS and is well established in literature today.

We know that in early years, the role of the adult is crucial in supporting separation anxiety and distress that children experience, when separated from their primary caregiver.

Introducing mindfulness activities and experiences over a period of time, such as 12 weeks, has shown greater improvements in children's social competence, health and emotional development (Flook and Goldbery, 2015).

In addition to the benefits of mindfulness to children's development and learning, research by Snyder et al. (2011) recognises that the transition to parenthood is often a stressful one in which attachment can be affected. They highlight the field of mindfulness as a practice shown to increase a mother's emotional regulation while decrease stress and anxiety. This shows mindfulness as an important contributing factor in healthy mother–child relationships, which recognises the potentially beneficial effects of mindfulness training on healthy attachment (Snyder et al., 2011).

Maslow's hierarchy of needs

Abraham Maslow introduced the concept that all human beings have a set of basic human needs. His hierarchy of needs model was developed in 1943 and is one of the best-known theories of motivation. It is depicted as a five-tier pyramid and is divided into basic needs (Levels 1 and 2); psychological needs (Levels 3 and 4) and self-fulfilment or growth needs (Level 5).

Level 5:
Self-
actualisation

Level 4: Esteem

Level 3: Love and social belonging

Level 2: Safety needs

Level 1: Physiological needs

Figure 1.7 **Maslow's hierarchy of needs pyramid.**

EYPs and EYTs are instrumental in supporting children to form secure attachments in the early years, and attuned to meeting the wider range of needs, as identified by Maslow in his 'Hierarchy of Needs' pyramid model. Maslow's theory suggests that these levels of needs support children's wellbeing and that each level builds upon the level below, as shown in this model.

This five-tier model can be reflected upon in your setting when considering children's individual needs. The EYFS sets the standards that early years settings must meet to ensure children learn, develop and are kept healthy and safe. The safeguarding and welfare requirements provide the steps that need to be followed to keep children safe and healthy, this meets their basic needs (Levels 1 and 2). The learning and development requirements and the development matters guidance shape the activities and experiences for children by identifying the goals children should be working towards to meet their psychological and self-fulfilment needs (Levels 3, 4 and 5).

It is important to remember that EYPs and EYTs apply this model not only to children but for themselves too, to support their own wellbeing, mental health and continuous development.

The teaching and modelling of mindfulness practices for children will enable EYPs and EYTs to relate to Maslow's theory with more awareness and compassion in supporting and nurturing each level of need.

It is important that professionals working with children have an awareness of Maslow's Hierarchy of needs, as these provide the wider context to identified behaviours, emotions and actions that can be supported for children's self-regulation and wellbeing. For example, if the basic needs (Levels 1 and 2) of a child are not met, the ability for them to manage their feelings, emotions, build trust and relationships may be affected.

The case study below provides our first look at the benefits of introducing mindfulness to children in an early year's environment.

Case Study: Day Nursery Setting

Saima, Early Years Practitioner

I am a qualified practitioner with ten years' experience of working with babies, toddlers and children. For this case study, I wanted to share my experience of using mindfulness practices with a group of pre-school children in my nursery setting. Supporting children's mental health and wellbeing is an important part of the curiosity approach that we use in the setting.

I started by introducing one to two mindfulness activities with a group of five children, asking them to visualise sitting on the beach and feeling the warm sand between their toes and noticing the warm sun shining down; also eating and tasting food mindfully, talking about the flavours and tastes of the fruit and vegetables on their plate; doing yoga and noticing their breathing and feelings. After a few weeks, I noticed a difference in how children were more focused, and they really liked practising sitting still and being 'mindful'. I shared this with some of the other staff, and as everyone is supportive, they gave it a go too.

Supporting children's emotional wellbeing has always been of interest to me, and so I spoke to my manager about my ideas and why I wanted to introduce mindfulness. To me this means to have inner peace for myself and support children learn about their feelings, because sometimes they can have very intense feelings which can lead to anger, frustration and emotional outbursts. My ideas were discussed at a staff meeting, and I shared some of the activities with the other staff. When planning the activities, I included a range that linked to the curriculum areas for social and emotional development with story-telling and mindful movements with a children's favourite 'Going on a Bear Hunt'.

As a result, we now have a 'mindful hour' in our setting, which really helps the children to sit, choose and do activities on their own or with others that improve their ability to be calm and more focused. Some choose to be mindful for five to ten minutes with the staff modelling and supporting, and this is really helping to build their concentration on one thing at a time.

The children enjoy doing yoga, mindful eating at mealtimes, belly breathing and listening to stories in the mindful hour.

As an adult working in early years, most days are very busy, so 'mindfulness hour' brings calmness and really helps support children to share their feelings and notice body movements and their breathing patterns. As adults we can model this to them, as a skill that they can develop for life. I realise mindfulness can help with supporting wellbeing, and working in a small team, we are all supportive and have different ideas that are planned from our observations and the children's needs.

Babies and children are learning to manage their emotions, and the best way to start is to introduce a small group of children to some simple daily mindfulness activities to encourage them to notice their feelings whilst sitting, moving or doing a task such as painting, drawing, yoga or music time. Introducing words such as 'breathe, calm, relax, breathe all the way down to your belly, be still and relax, how do you feel today?' starts to increase children's vocabulary and understanding of 'what is calm' and how it feels in their body and mind. The best time of day for the children varied; however, I noticed that after breakfast and before sleeping/rest time worked well when there is natural quiet time.

My reason for introducing mindfulness was that children needed more time to sit, relax and have quieter moments. Mindfulness works best early morning and after lunch when there is natural quiet time. It is also effective when helping children to manage their emotions if something is making them upset, angry or they are tired.

Impact: The impact is that the children are more calm, more engaged in activities and more understanding of each other's needs and feelings. Staff working together to model and support this has really helped. I have noticed that there are less behaviour issues as the environment is less chaotic. The children are teaching each other yoga and breathing indoors and outdoors. Feedback to and from parents is positive and they are happy with mindfulness in the routine. I would suggest that all settings try mindfulness by introducing it for at least ten to fifteen minutes per day and then increase this, as mindfulness activities support children's social and emotional skills.

Conclusion

This chapter introduced the aims and rationale of this book. It provided a scope for each chapter and introduced the reader to some simple mindful exercises for themselves and for children. Definitions of mindfulness, wellbeing, mental health and self-regulation were explored and the origins of mindfulness explained. A key focus of the chapter was to introduce what mindfulness is, how this practice has been introduced into the field of education, with the growing research base for mindfulness discussed in providing a rationale for its implementation into early years provision.

The benefits of mindfulness practices in supporting children's mental health, wellbeing and fostering self-regulation skills, essential for early childhood were explained, with some simple mindful practices and reflective activities support knowledge, awareness and understanding. Links to the EYFS and relevance of mindfulness as a practice to support children's mental health, as recognised by parliament and welcomed by Ofsted.

References

Allen, G. (2011) *Early intervention:* The next steps. Accessed 14 May 2021 at https://www.gov.uk/government/publications/early-intervention-the-next-steps--2

Bishop, S., et al. (2004) Mindfulness: A Proposed Operational Definition. Accessed on 28 June 2021 at https://www.integrativehealthpartners.org/downloads/Bishop_et_al.pdf

Boyce, B. (2018) *Defining Mindfulness.* Accessed on 18 January 2023 at https://www.mindful.org/defining-mindfulness/

Burke, C. (2009) *Mindfulness-Based Approaches with Children and Adolescents: A Preliminary Review of Current Research in an Emergent Field.* Accessed on 15 November 2021 at https://www.researchgate.net/publication/330358657_Mindfulness-Based_Approaches_with_Children_and_Adolescents_A_Preliminary_Review_of_Current_Research_in_an_Emergent_Field

Capel, C. (2012) Mindlessness/mindfulness, classroom practices and quality of early childhood education: An auto-ethnographic and intrinsic case research. International Journal of Quality & Reliability Management 29(6) 666–680 Accessed on 5 June 2023 at https://www.researchgate.net/publication/235279727_Mindlessnessmindfulness_classroom_practices_and_quality_of_early_childhood_education_An_auto-ethnographic_and_intrinsic_case_research

Cherry, K. (2019) *What is Attachment Theory? The Importance of Early Emotional Bonds.* Accessed on 27 July 2021 at https://www.verywellmind.com/what-is-attachment-theory-2795337#:~:text=Attachment%20is%20an%20emotional%20bond,the%20child's%20chances%20of%20survival

Conkbayir, M. (2020) *Self-Regulation in Early Years.* Accessed on 12 July 2021 at https://eyfs.info/articles.html/personal-social-and-emotional-development/self-regulation-in-early-years-r283/

Currid, J. (2020) *Mindfulness in Early Learning and Care.* Accessed on 12 June 2021 at https://knowledge.barnardos.ie/handle/20.500.13085/189

Cvitković, D. (2021) *The role of yoga in education.* Accessed on 5 June 2023 at https://www.researchgate.net/publication/356147572_THE_ROLE_OF_YOGA_IN_EDUCATION

Department for Education (DfE) (2021) *Development Matters Guidance Non-statutory Curriculum Guidance for the Early Years Foundation Stage.* Accessed on 4 February 2022 at https://assets.publishing.service.gov.uk/government/uploads/system/uploads/attachment_data/file/1007446/6.7534_DfE_Development_Matters_Report_and_illustrations_web__2_.pdf

Department of Health (2012) *National Survey of Investment in Adult Mental Health Services.* Accessed on 4 November 2021 at https://assets.publishing.service.gov.uk/government/uploads/system/uploads/attachment_data/file/140098/FinMap2012-NatReportAdult-0308212.pdf

Dinehart, L. and Willis, E., (2013) *Contemplative Practices in Early Childhood: Implications for Self-regulation Skills and School Readiness.* Accessed on 23 July 2021 at https://www.tandfonline.com/doi/full/10.1080/03004430.2013.804069?needAccess=true

Early Years Alliance (2021) *Changes to the EYFS 2021.* Accessed on 5 July 2021 at https://www.eyalliance.org.uk/changes-eyfs-2021

Erwin, E. and Robinson, K., (2015) *The Joy of Being: Making Way for Young Children's Natural Mindfulness.* Accessed on 24 May 2021 at https://www.montclair.edu/profilepages/media/1948/user/erwinrobinsinon2015joyofbeinginpdf.pdf

Flook, L., Goldberg, S., Pinger, L., Davidson, R. (2014) *Promoting Prosocial Behavior and Self-Regulatory Skills in Preschool Children Through a Mindfulness-Based Kindness Curriculum.* Developmental Psychology, Vol. 51, No. 1, 44 –51 Accessed on 5 June 2023 at https://www.researchgate.net/publication/268154782_Promoting_Prosocial_Behavior_and_Self-Regulatory_Skills_in_Preschool_Children_Through_a_Mindfulness-Based_Kindness_Curriculum

Fossas, A. (2015) *The Basics of Mindfulness: Where Did It Come From?* Accessed on 2 May 2021 at https://welldoing.org/article/basics-of-mindfulness-come-from

Jones, D. (2011) Mindfulness in Schools. Accessed on 2 July 2022 at https://www.bps.org.uk/psychologist/mindfulness-schools

Kabat-Zinn, J. (1990) *Full Catastrophe Living: Using the Wisdom of your Body and Mind to Face Stress, Pain, and Illness.* Delacorte Press: New York.

Kabat-Zinn, J. (2003) 'Mindfulness-Based Interventions in Context: Past, Present and Future', *Clinical Psychology: Science and Practice,* 10, pp. 144–156.

Laevers, F. (2005) *Experiential Education-Deep Level Learning in Early Childhood and Primary Education. University of Leuven.* Accessed on 25 February 2021 at http://www.speelsleren.nl/wp-content/uploads/2015/05/Deep-level-learning-Ferre-Laevers.pdf

Mental Health Foundation (2016) *Fundamental Facts about Mental Health.* Accessed on 23 July 2021 at https://www.mentalhealth.org.uk/sites/default/files/2022-06/The-Fundamental-facts-about-mental-health-2016.pdf

Mental Health Foundation (2022) *Good Mental Health for All.* Accessed on 15 July 2021 at https://www.mentalhealth.org.uk/

Mental Health of Children and Young People in England (2020) *Wave 1 Follow Up to the 2017 Survey (Published October 2020).* Accessed on 8 December 2021 at https://digital.nhs.uk/data-and-information/publications/statistical/mental-health-of-children-and-young-people-in-england

Mentally Healthy Schools (2021) *Attachment and Child Development.* Accessed on 18 February 2021 at https://mentallyhealthyschools.org.uk/mental-health-needs/attachment-and-child-development/

Mind (2015) Cited in Professional Association for Childcare and Early Years (PACEY) (2015) *The Role of Childcare Professionals in Supporting Mental Health and Wellbeing in Young People: A Literature Review.* Accessed on 15 November 2021 at https://www.pacey.org.uk/Pacey/media/Website-files/PACEY%20general/Emotional-wellbeing_literaturereview_Dec2015.pdf

Mindfulness All Party Parliamentary Group (MAPPG) (2015) *Mindful Nation UK Report.* Accessed on 26 November 2021 at https://www.themindfulnessinitiative.org/mindful-nation-report

Mineo, L. (2018) *With Mindfulness, Life's in the Moment.* Accessed on 18 December 2022 at https://news.harvard.edu/gazette/story/2018/04/less-stress-clearer-thoughts-with-mindfulness-meditation/

Moss, S. (2012) Natural Childhood by Stephen Moss 2012 – National Trust Report. Accessed on 10 May 2021 at https://www.outdoor-learning-research.org/Research/Research-Blog/Art MID/560/ArticleID/24/Natural-Childhood-by-Stephen-Moss-2012-National-Trust-Report

Mukadam, Y. and Sutherland, H. (2018) *Supporting Toddlers' Wellbeing in Early Years Settings.* London: Jessica Kingsley Publishers.

Nadler, R., et al. (2017). 'A Brief Mindfulness Practice Increases Self-Reported Calmness in Young Children: A Pilot Study', *Mindfulness,* 8(4), pp. 1088–1095.

Naylor, C., Parsonage, M., McDaid, D., Knapp, M., Fossey, M., Galea, A. (2012) *Long-Term Conditions and Mental Health: The Cost of Co-Morbidities.* Accessed on 14 April 2021 at https://eprints.lse.ac.uk/41873/

National Health Service (NHS) (2022) *Mindful.* Accessed on 1 October 2020 at https://www.nhs.uk/mental-health/self-help/tips-and-support/mindfulness/#:~:text=Mindfulness%20meditation%20involves%20sitting%20silently,the%20mind%20starts%20to%20wander

National Health Service (NHS) (2017) *Mental Health of Children and Young People, 2017.* Accessed on 15 November 2022 at https://digital.nhs.uk/data-and-information/publications/statistical/mental-health-of-children-and-young-people-in-england/2017/2017

National Health Service (NHS) Digital (2020) *Mental Health of Children and Young People in England, 2020, Wave 1 Follow Up to the 2017 Survey.* Accessed on 12 January 2023 at https://files.digital.nhs.uk/AF/AECD6B/mhcyp_2020_rep_v2.pdf

New Economics Foundation (NEF) (2014) *Wellbeing Economics Report.* Accessed on 28 March 2021 at https://wellbeingeconomics.co.uk/wp-content/uploads/2018/11/appg-report-2014.pdf

Pickert, K. (2014) *Time Magazine: The Mindful Revolution.* Accessed on 4 September 2021 at https://time.com/1556/the-mindful-revolution/

Shanker, S. (2017) *Self-Regulation: The Early Years.* Accessed on 15 January 2022 at https://self-reg.ca/wp-content/uploads/2021/05/infosheet_The-Early-Years.pdf

Shanker, S. (2021) *Self-Regulation in the Early Years.* Accessed on 16 January 2022 at https://self-reg.ca/self-reg-in-the-early-years/

Snyder, R., Shapiro, S. and Treleaven, D. (2011) *Attachment Theory and Mindfulness.* Accessed on 29 May 2021 at https://www.researchgate.net/publication/257578367_Attachment_Theory_and_Mindfulness

Statham, J. and Chase, E. (2010) *Childhood Wellbeing: A Brief Overview.* Accessed on 12 February 2021 at https://assets.publishing.service.gov.uk/government/uploads/system/uploads/attachment_data/file/183197/Child-Wellbeing-Brief.pdf

The Awake Network (2018) Mindful Education Summit. Accessed on 21 November 2018 at https://www.theawakenetwork.com/my-library/bonus-series/7-day-mindful-living-series/

The Children's Society (2016) *The Good Child Report 2016.* Accessed on 4 June 2022 at https://www.basw.co.uk/system/files/resources/basw_94045-10_0.pdf

The Mindfulness Initiative (2015) *Mindful Nation UK Report.* Accessed on 5 May 2021 at https://www.themindfulnessinitiative.org/Handlers/Download.ashx?IDMF=1af56392-4cf1-4550-bdd1-72e809fa627a

Titmuss, C. (2014) *Mindfulness for Everyday Living. Barrons Educational Series Inc.*

Trousselard et al. (2014) Cited in *History of Mindfulness: From East to West and Religion to Science.* Accessed on 17 November 2021 at https://positivepsychology.com/history-of-mindfulness/

UNICEF (2000) *A League Table of Child Poverty in Rich Nations.* Accessed on 26 October 2021 at https://www.unicef-irc.org/publications/226-a-league-table-of-child-poverty-in-rich-nations.html

UNICEF (2007) *Child Poverty in Perspective: An Overview of Child Well-Being in Rich Countries, Innocenti Report Card, No. 7.* Accessed on 12 May 2022 at https://www.unicef-irc.org/article/552-innocenti-report-card-7-an-overview-of-child-well-being-in-rich-countries.html

UNICEF (2013) *Report Card 11: Child Well-Being in Rich Countries.* Accessed on 15 September 2021 at https://www.unicef-irc.org/research/report-card-11/

Wbur (2018) *Meditation in the Mainstream: The Growing Mindfulness Movement.* Accessed on 26 October 2021 at https://www.wbur.org/onpoint/2018/08/14/meditation-mindfulness-jon-kabat-zinn

Weare, K. (2013) 'Developing Mindfulness with Children and Young People: A Review of the Evidence and Policy context', *Journal of Children's Services*, 8(2), pp. 141–153.https://doi.org/10.1108/JCS-12-2012-0014

Wedge, M. (2018) *7 Ways Mindfulness Can Help Children's Brains.* Accessed on 4 June 2020 at https://www.psychologytoday.com/gb/blog/suffer-the-children/201809/7-ways-mindfulness-can-help-children-s-brains

World Health Organization (WHO) (2014) Mental Health: A State of Well-Being. Accessed on 18 May 2022 at https://www.who.int/features/factfiles/mental_health/en

World Health Organization (WHO) (2022) *Technical Brief: Improving Mental Health Is a Priority for Public Health, Human Rights and Sustainable Development.* Accessed on 16 January 2023 at https://cdn.who.int/media/docs/default-source/universal-health-coverage/who-uhl-technical-brief—mental-health.pdf?sfvrsn=3630b9a1_3&download=true

2 The mindful pedagogy

Aims of Chapter 2

This chapter aims to:

■ Define the term mindfulness pedagogy.
■ Explore approaches that inform the mindful pedagogy approach.
■ Develop a mindful pedagogy for your early year's practice.
■ Understand the role of neuroscience and early brain development to inform a mindful pedagogy in your setting.

Introduction

This chapter explores the term 'mindful pedagogy' and illustrates what this means in theory as well as practice. It will identify why pedagogy is important and how a mindful pedagogical approach can be planned and implemented in your early years setting.

Definitions of the terms mindfulness and pedagogy will be explored as a first step in determining the key principles of a mindful pedagogy for your provision. Alongside this, we will consider and identify a child–centred philosophy to strengthen a more mindful approach to teaching and learning.

The early years foundation stage (EYFS) and some well-known pedagogical approaches will inform the mindful pedagogy for your practice, and underpinned by one of the four EYFS principles, the 'Unique Child' which states that 'Every child is a unique child, who is constantly learning and can be resilient, capable, confident and self-assured' (DfE, 2012). Strategies for developing a mindful pedagogy and its impact on children's wellbeing and development are explored, through the growing field of neuroscience research, the limbic system and early brain development.

DOI: 10.4324/9780429030734-3

Early years play and pedagogy

As we know, effective EYPs and EYTs plan and implement appropriate learning for children, and the role of the adult is dependent upon the pedagogical approaches implemented within the early years setting, which support children's emotional well-being, self-regulation skills and mental health.

The word 'pedagogy' is a term that is not readily used by policymakers or within the early years sector. Therefore, to clarify from the outset, pedagogy is essentially the theory and practice of *how adults lead children to learn* through planned approaches, strategies and interactions in the setting.

Arnerich (2021) identifies that pedagogy is the 'how' of teaching and involves how professionals in early years educate and support early childhood development. He adds that it also includes strategies and techniques that provide opportunities for early learning and the importance of establishing positive relationships and interactions with children.

You will be aware that, it is through play that children absorb their surroundings and make sense of the world around them, and that early years practitioners (EYPs) and early years teachers (EYTs) respond to each child's emerging needs and interests, guiding their development through warm, positive interactions (DfE, 2012).

The value of play and its relevance has been embedded into early year's philosophy through pioneers such as Froebel, Steiner and Dewey, who have helped to lay the strong foundations for play as central to promoting and supporting children's learning (Nutbrown et al., 2008 cited in Johnson (2014).

There remains a tension between the need to provide a purposeful play-based curriculum and not ignoring the requirement for school readiness. In doing so, this dual responsibility of early years professionals reminds us that 'pedagogy encompasses both what practitioners actually do and think, and the principles, theories, perceptions and challenges that inform and shape it' (Moyles et al., 2002, p. 5).

Developing a mindful pedagogy

For developing a mindful pedagogy in your setting, there needs to be a clear vision of why mindfulness is important alongside play. It is important for EYPs and EYTs to clarify the vision by reflecting on the following key areas when considering the pedagogy in the setting:

Children's behaviour – Awareness of how the child's daily routine and experiences shape their behaviour and emotions. Are there effective strategies and policies in place to support positive behaviour management as well as self-regulation?

Child development – Do all adults understand how children learn and develop? Do they have knowledge of the development and emotional milestones of the first five years of life?

Figure 2.1 **Girl lying on tummy in a field, hand on chin.**

Brain development – What is the understanding and knowledge base of adults working with children regarding how the brain develops before the baby is born and through early childhood?

Relationships – How are relationships supported and developed, particularly during times of change and transitions experienced by children in the home and early years environment?

Addressing these key areas of pedagogy can enable EYPs and EYTs to fully understand and endorse a mindful pedagogical approach by applying these building blocks.

This definition further supports our understanding of the term pedagogy:

Pedagogy refers to that set of instructional techniques and strategies which enable learning to take place and provide opportunities for the acquisition of knowledge, skills, attitudes and dispositions within a particular social and material context

(Siraj-Blatchford et al., 2002)

To put this into context, key findings from the Department for Education (DfE) (2015) research brief in early childhood identified several strengths of the pedagogy in England, which are as follows:

1. England's pedagogical approach in the EYFS curriculum puts emphasis on age-appropriateness and play in pedagogy and encourages staff to employ different approaches and practices flexibly.

   The theories of Piaget and Vygotsky are frequently mentioned to have influenced pedagogy and curriculum in England.

2. Along with Denmark, Germany and New Zealand, England promotes continuous child development for the whole early childhood education and care (ECEC) age range due to implementation of one over-arching curriculum framework.

3. Thirdly, England has favourable staff-child ratios in place that can positively impact pedagogy, as this determines how much time practitioners can spend per child. England and Finland have the most favourable staff-child ratios in place for children below the age of three.

In practice, many early years settings in England employ a combination of pedagogical approaches and do not subscribe to an exclusive approach; however, a child-centred approach is popular and implemented in many settings in countries such as England, Denmark and Germany applying a more interactive (constructivist) approach.

Many international studies recognise that children's achievements are shaped by the quality of the pedagogical interactions between the staff and children in the setting, as well as between peers, and with their environment. The studies show that these interactions and experiences are one of the most significant factors in supporting children's learning and development (DfE, 2015).

Today, the unique child commitment (1.4) to promote the health and well-being of children is a focused priority at both macro and micro level. Before exploring how mindfulness can be adopted as an approach in your early years setting, it is important to now understand the meaning of the terms 'mindfulness' alongside 'pedagogy' and the value of this approach for early years settings.

Explore the term mindful pedagogy

Mindful pedagogy is a term you may or not be familiar with in your work. Before we begin to explore and talk about the purpose and benefits of a mindful pedagogy and what this looks like in early years practice, we need to understand what the terms 'mindfulness' and 'pedagogy' means.

The term **mindfulness** has many definitions (as discussed in Chapter 1); however, the common thread in each definition is the ability to slow down our thoughts, becoming more aware of them whilst consciously existing in present moment awareness for as long as our mind is able to. This is why mindfulness activities and practices often intentionally focus on the breath or suggest an insightful presence to an activity.

Focusing on the breath is a key facet of present moment awareness. Mindfulness enables an individual to slow down their thoughts and to be in the present moment, with curiosity and awareness of what is happening around them without any judgment. Mindfulness practices are often an intentional and systemic way of developing values of compassion and kindness into everyday activities. John Kabat-Zinn coined the term Mindfulness, defining it as 'paying attention in a particular way: on purpose, in the present moment, and non-judgmentally' (Kabat-Zinn, 1990). With this idea in mind, neuroscience tells us about the transient nature of our thoughts and emotions which mindfulness practice allows us to connect with.

Put simply, pedagogy is about how we educate children and help their development. It is about the techniques and strategies, and the effective relationships and interactions to support development (Arnerich, 2018)

The term **pedagogy** can be defined as the approach taken to impart teaching and learning of individuals within any learning environment such as an early year's classroom, day care setting or other training establishment. The pedagogy can be moulded and adapted to fit the core values, aims and philosophy of an organisation. The DfE (2015) *define pedagogy as 'how' we educate children. Furthermore, pedagogy is referred to as:*

> that set of instructional techniques and strategies which enable learning to take place…and the interactive process between teacher, learner and the learning environment
>
> (Siraj-Blatchford, 2002)

Therefore, the term **mindful pedagogy** is a way of teaching and learning that embeds **principles of mindfulness** which for early years are:

1. **The wellbeing of staff and children in the setting:** the aim is to nurture in children a sense of wellbeing, self-regulation and self-esteem. The curriculum should aim to create a climate that facilitates children and practitioner's emotional wellbeing.

2. **Create a mindful environment setting wide:** a child-centred approach to daily practices reflected within a mindful learning environment (i.e. calm, happy places for children to experience), where children and practitioners can build and enjoy a community that understands the concept of mindfulness.

3. **Create a curriculum that interconnects between learning and mindfulness:** supporting children to thrive and become life-long learners with a strong sense of self and a positive outlook on life by engaging in activities and building relationships.

Understanding a mindful pedagogy in theory and in practice

In **theory**, a mindful pedagogy can be defined by the DfE (2015) as 'how' we educate children. The mindfulness element is always present if practitioners apply the fundamental principles of mindfulness to their daily approach emphasised by Siraj-Blatchford (2002) as 'that set of instructional techniques and strategies which enable learning to take pace… and the interactive process between teacher, learner and the learning environment'.

With growing research in building the case for mindfulness, Taggart (2015, p. 385) suggests that a 'mindful attitude may help to promote "tuning into children and help practitioners to be present" with them whilst also resisting the anxious and exhausted thinking which arises from such continuous emotional support'. Evidence from his research confirmed that 90% ($n = 17$) of early years practitioner students studying for an MA, claimed to be 'more available to the children if their minds were less pre-occupied'. This was in direct response to two specific questions relating to mindfulness within the research.

The research from my research (see case study in chapter 6) with a group of teachers identified the beneficial outcomes of Mindfulness-Based Stress Reduction (MBSR) training programme to improve 'attentiveness', 'calm' and 'presence' to their own teaching and wellbeing. Three teachers emphasised that 'the shared learning experience enabled them to express their feelings and emotions within a safe environment' where a member of the senior leadership team was present, therefore impacting positively on their future workload, wellbeing and stress levels.

In **practice**, a mindful pedagogy can be influenced and made up of a range of existing pedagogical approaches that early years settings have chosen to adopt alongside the EYFS curriculum expectations. We will start by determining what we mean by early years pedagogy, then go on to explore some of the well-known pedagogies and their impact on children's learning and development.

An early years pedagogy is how practitioners and teachers educate children to support their learning and development (Mukadam and Kaur, 2016). When shifting our focus to the term *mindfulness pedagogy*, the main emphasis is for practitioners to facilitate and scaffold children's learning and support their ability to self-regulate. Veale (2016) suggests that, practitioners need to apply effective pedagogical approaches that combine the notion of children's curiosity alongside guided adult interactions that support and enhance learning and development opportunities.

To enable the mindful pedagogical approach requires practitioners to move away from 'the expectations of product-orientated learning and school readiness to a more holistic approach that offers meaningful and enjoyable learning experiences suited to children's abilities and interests', (Veale, 2016) and include the follow key components:

1. Meeting personal, social and emotional needs in order to enhance social competencies for life.

2. Introducing and role modelling mindfulness techniques and strategies to manage daily stressors.

3. Supporting children to self-regulate by effectively supporting them to manage their emotions, and coaching them to manage their behaviours in response to daily stressors in their routine.

4. Co-regulation and coaching children supports mindfulness and self-regulation (Rouse, 2020). He suggests that adult guidance ensures 'not to avoid situations that are difficult for children to handle, but to provide a supportive framework and scaffold the behaviour you want to encourage, until they can handle these challenges on their own'.

The purpose of a mindful pedagogy is to connect children's wellbeing as a main component in supporting their learning and future academic achievement. Therefore, when planning and facilitating children's care, learning and development, a mindfulness pedagogy can be achieved through reflection upon four points that are underpinned to the theme, 'A Unique Child' and its subsequent commitments.

Activity

Consider the four focus points in Table 2.1, then identify how these will apply in practice as you develop your mindful pedagogy.

Table 2.1   Focus Areas to Develop Your Mindful Pedagogy

Theme: unique child	Focus points for mindful pedagogy	How will this apply in practice?
1.1 Child development	Point 1: Get to know the child, aim not to suppress their natural tendencies and aptitudes; understand their stage of development	
1.2 Inclusive practice	Point 2: Support learning when the child is ready respecting the diversity of individuals; experiential learning as the dominant mode.	
1.3 Keeping safe	Point 3: Support their basis needs and maintain a safe environment to build resilience; meet physical and psychological needs.	
1.4 Health and wellbeing	Point 4: Co-regulate to support the child to manage their emotions.	

Pedagogical approaches

Here are some well-known early year's pedagogical approaches that you may be familiar with and currently implementing within your practice. Consider aspects of these for the Mindful Pedagogy that you will develop later in the chapter.

The Swedish Curriculum idealises on play and natural explorations. Children develop independence from the outset that prepares them with essential skills required for later life such as self-help and self-awareness. The learning environment created by the 'Pedagogue' is home like and based upon creating a natural environment where the outdoors is the primary environment for learning. Children spend half of the day outdoors regardless of weather conditions, with babies sleeping outdoors as fresh air benefits healthy development. The curriculum is based on three prime aspects: challenge, discovery and adventure. Each experience is based on a quest for fun rather than learning. This philosophy is shared equally by both the parents and the Pedagogues. The adult's role is to deliver the curriculum in a way that interests them rather than led by statutory drivers and outcomes.

The Montessori Approach of education is a widely followed approach which helps children to achieve their maximum potential within a structured learning environment. Maria Montessori pioneered 'discovery learning' which meant that her philosophy was that children are born with an innate capacity to absorb ideas and language within their environment. Montessori developed a structured education programme based upon the developmental stages of a child. She devised special equipment called 'didactic' materials which meant 'intended to instruct'. The aim of this type of learning was to engage children to foster a life-long motivation for learning. This approach suggest that play should have a learning focus.

The Reggio Emilia Approach originated in Italy after the Second World War.

Loris Malaguzzi was the founder of this parent initiated led and driven approach to provide effective learning experiences for pre-school children. This is a classic example of a process-driven approach whereby the curriculum remains fluid, emergent and stems from the child's own unique interests and curiosity. The role of the 'Teacher' is primarily as 'observer' then documenter and finally a partner in the learning process for each child. The 'Teacher' facilitates children to become active learners irrespective of their age or stage of development. The environment is considered as the 'third teacher' besides parents and teachers. A well-lit, well-ventilated and orderly environment promotes a sense of well-being which helps children to delve in new learning and discover new experiences.

The high-scope curriculum

The high-scope curriculum is based on Piaget's intellectual development theory. The main elements of this approach are similar to the EYFS. The key of high scope is the Plan-Do-Review cycle where children are involved in planning their own play followed by its implementation and reflection on it.

The five dimensions of 'school readiness' are the key principles and include: approaches to learning; language; literacy and communication; social and emotional development; physical development; health and well-being; arts and sciences. This curriculum focuses on active participative learning where teachers and practitioners are as active and engaged as the children. Adults provide a learning environment that promotes independence, curiosity, decision-making, co-operation, persistence, creativity and problem solving.

Children learn how to act with intentions and reflect on the consequences of their actions. There is a shared control in adult–child interactions and this provides a balance of freedom that children need to explore with the limits for them to feel secure.

The Te Whariki Curriculum was established in New Zealand in 1996 as a bicultural, holistic curriculum. It was regulated in 2008 with a positivist approach taken by the workforce with its implementation. This curriculum promotes active participation of adults and embraces teachers, practitioners and parents in children's learning and development. The ideology of the curriculum is the weaving of the following four principles: empowerment, holistic development, family and community and relationships in children's early life experiences to prepare them for secure development. When compared with the EYFS, this curriculum reflects a similar philosophy.

Keys aims of a mindful pedagogy

A mindful pedagogy is an approach that begins with staff getting to know each child, then creating a fit for purpose physical and emotional environment and appropriate experiences that support their mental health and wellbeing. Scaffolding and modelling skills enables children to develop a mindful approach to their daily routine, with knowledgeable adults who can co-regulate and support children to manage their feelings and emotions in a supportive environment. This can further lead onto building friendships and relationships with the key person and peers, as they learn to empathise with others, gain independence and develop confidence and a sense of belonging. Here are four key aims to consider as a staff team or group when developing your mindful pedagogy:

- **Aim 1: Culture** – An important first step is for staff to adapt a more mindful culture in the way that they think, communicate, behave and celebrate cultural differences within the setting. There will be families from a wide variety of cultures, therefore acknowledging and celebrating cultural diversity is important. For example, holidays, festivals, clothing, language and what we eat.

- **Aim 2: Development** – The next step is for the staff to focus on a change management *process* towards a more mindful pedagogy, which is centred around each child's needs and upheld by an understanding of working in a more present moment early years environment. Understanding the pattern of children's development.

- **Aim 3: Behaviour** – A relational approach to nurturing positive behaviour aligns with the staff being mindful in understanding the needs of children in the present moment. These supportive interactions that children experience will shape their behaviour and ability to manage stressors.

■ **Aim 4: Relationships** – The successful implementation depends on the skillset and knowledge of staff to adapt and design the teaching, learning, environment (pedagogical approach) that helps children change and learn in relation to those around them.

The key thing to remember here is that the effectiveness of the pedagogy depends on the commitment and understanding of the practitioners and teachers and their integrity to ensure that a mindful approach to care and learning is embedded into the core of their teaching and care of all children. Therefore, the personal values and beliefs of staff and teachers must be aligned to core aims of the pedagogy above. Also, if the philosophy does not align, then it will be challenging to work in an environment that is focused on children's attainment rather than focusing on wellbeing or building relationships.

Benefits of a mindful pedagogy

The main benefit of developing a mindful pedagogy is to consciously create a more nurturing, natural and calming environment and routine.

In addition, other key benefits over a period of time are:

■ Mindful adults who are skilled in managing their own state, and in doing so are more in tune with supporting children to manage their feelings, emotions and wellbeing needs.

■ A collaborative approach to working provides a supportive environment and ultimately a harmonised and calmer learning environment.

■ A caring culture is developed from welcoming children and families, engaging with children during the routine with a more child-centred and playful approach that meets the individual needs of all children.

Creating the mindful pedagogy

There are many pedagogies to choose from in early years. It is often beneficial to consider aspects from various pedagogies and create one that is fit for purpose in your particular setting.

The pedagogies described are not necessarily conflicting one another in their purpose, instead they provide concepts, principles of practice and particular focus areas central to their philosophy. When creating your mindful pedagogy, you need to do the same and maintain the child's individual needs and emotional wellbeing as a central focus.

We have now discussed the EYFS and its purpose, understood the terms mindful and pedagogy and explored a range of pedagogical approaches influencing the EYFS. You are now able to develop a fit for purpose mindful pedagogy for your setting and practice.

Notes: ....
....
....
....

Activity

Review the questions in Table 2.2 and note down any comments that may be helpful when formulating your pedagogical approach for supporting children's mental health and wellbeing.

Table 2.2   Review Questions and Notes for Your Pedagogical Approach

Areas to consider	*Comments*
Learning and development: How can adults plan and provide a daily routine that recognises a more mindful wellbeing approach whilst considering the unique needs of all children?	
What will a daily mindful pedagogy look like in your setting?	
As professionals introducing mindful strategies and techniques, what is the outcome you would like to achieve?	
How effectively can the mindful pedagogy support learning and development of children's self-regulation skills and build resilience?	
Behaviour: How will more mindful learning experiences shape children's positive behaviour?	
How can setting policy reflect a more relational approach to recognise children's emotions and feelings in a safe environment?	
What constitutes mindful staff? For example, how will staff focus on the child rather than the curriculum?	
Relationships: With a mindful learning environment, how will children be supported to adapt and build trusting relationships with other children and adults?	
What will be the benefits to the child and the setting for enabling positive relationships?	
How will you create a more calm, responsive, accepting and caring environment? (key pillars)	
Culture: How can family life and culture be embraced to enhance wellbeing and impact positively on learning and relationships?	

Essentially, children's learning and development is dependent on the pedagogical approaches that practitioners use in the setting, and it is not uncommon for early year's settings to use a variety of pedagogical approaches. What is implemented is dependent on the familiarity or preferred pedagogies of practitioners and the teachers; or what is common practice in a particular school or day care setting, as opposed to developing a pedagogy around the children and their needs.

A DfE Research Brief (2015, p. 7) about early year's pedagogy indicated that 'it is important that pedagogy remains child-centred, and developmentally appropriate, with an emphasis on play-based learning'. Therefore, it is important for the staff team to critique current practices and identify areas for change with a strong rationale for adopting a mindful pedagogy that is child centred where the quality of interactions between adults and children plays a fundamental role in supporting learning. With statistics showing that anxiety and depression in children has risen by 40% since 2004 (Young Minds), it is important to develop practices that consider these statistics to inform future practices accordingly.

The EYFS and a mindful pedagogical approach

In the UK, the EYFS remains the statutory framework that sets the standards for the development, learning and care of children from birth to five. Effective care, teaching and learning relies on the knowledge, experiences and expertise of practitioners and the philosophy of the setting. A positive aspect of the EYFS framework is the flexibility to enable EYPs and EYTs to embed mindfulness where appropriate into the daily curriculum.

With children's mental health now more so at the forefront of children's wellbeing, self-regulation is more central to the EYFS. Therefore, a mindful centred pedagogy will enable EYPs and EYTs to focus on activities and techniques that enhance opportunities for children's wellbeing.

The Children's Society (2018) recognise that 5–10% of children in the UK have low wellbeing, suggesting that their basic needs are not being met. NSPCC Learning (2021) affirm a key message by from (Public Health England, 2021) that 'promoting children and young people's wellbeing is a key part of keeping them safe, helping them develop and ensuring they have positive outcomes into adulthood. This perspective aligns with the government's view that promoting wellbeing is important during the early years of a child's life as this can impact on their mental health as they get older (Moriarty, 2018).

For example, practitioners can measure wellbeing through the intervention of a circle time to discuss children's emotions and thoughts that day, supporting a simple yet effective daily mindfulness practice. This activity enables children to express their emotions, feelings and ideas within a safe environment, where trusting adults (practitioners) can understand each child's individual needs and support them to communicate their needs, problem solve and manage their feelings and emotions.

Creating a new approach, such as the Mindful Pedagogy, can take time unless the focus is clear and aligned by everyone participating. As stated in the Development Matters guidance (DfE, 2020), an effective pedagogy is a mix of different approaches where children learn through play and where adults model, guide learning and direct teaching. The Development Matters can support in developing further an approach that builds on the strengths and meet the emotional needs of the children.

Building your philosophy

Alongside the aims, the success of a mindful pedagogy and practice is a sound philosophy. Hawn (2023) states that 'children are our most precious resource for a happier, healthier tomorrow', therefore your philosophy should have emotional wellbeing at its core. Daniel Goleman's four pillars of emotional intelligence can strengthen the emotional context of your philosophy and are:

1. Self-awareness

2. Self-regulation

3. Empathy

4. Social skills

Activity

Discuss the following questions with others in your setting or professional network:

1. Which pedagogical approach do you most favour and why?

2. Which approaches inform your setting practice?

3. How can a Mindfulness Pedagogy benefit the children in your setting? (e.g. to improve emotional wellbeing, opportunities to be calm, compassionate, express feelings, feel nurtured, etc.)

....

....

....

Another way to effectively embed a mindful approach to the daily routine and the pedagogy in your early years setting is to have the right attitude and mindset. The **seven Attitudes of Mindfulness** developed by Jon Kabat-Zinn in the 1990s enables practitioners to make mindfulness a regular practice in the setting.

Activity

Reflect on each of these attitudes and consider how you can develop these in your professional role:

1. **Non-judging:** Noticing when you are being judgmental of yourself and others.

2. **Patience:** Letting things unfold in their own time without rushing.

3. **Beginner's Mind:** Being receptive to new possibilities and realising you don't need to know all the answers.

4. **Trust:** Trusting in yourself and taking responsibility for your actions.

5. **Non-Striving:** Not forcing certain results to happen and letting things happen in their own time.

6. **Acceptance:** Accepting things as they are in the moment without denying or trying to change things.

7. **Letting Go:** Being willing to let go of the things, people, or ideas that prevent you from living in the moment.

Notes:...

....

....

....

....

The main benefit of the mindful pedagogy is to consciously create a more nurturing, natural and calming environment and routine, where staff are able to apply these seven attitudes within daily practice. We know this type of approach is more important than ever before, with the findings from the Children's Mental Health

Report (Child Mind Institute, 2020a) identifying a decline in well-being since the coronavirus pandemic with,

■ More than two thirds of parents who sought help since the start of the pandemic saying they had witnessed a decline in their child's emotional well-being (72%), behaviour (68%) and physical health due to decreased activities/exercise (68%).

The Child Mind Institute (2020a, 2020b) also reported that the pandemic has been challenging for children and teenagers, especially those already dealing with mental health challenges.

Formulating a personal philosophy

Introducing mindfulness to young children is both a skill and a way of being. A philosophy grounded in this understanding will help you see that mindfulness can be a practical tool as well as skill to support emotional wellbeing now and in later life.

Creating a personal philosophy will enable you to establish a clear aim for your mindfulness pedagogy. A philosophy rooted in your own values and beliefs will enable you to work towards creating a pedagogy, environment and curriculum that supports your philosophical aspiration.

Activity

Answer these questions to start creating your philosophy:

1. Is my philosophy child-centred?
2. Does it consider the needs of all children?
3. Is it more focused on outcomes or children's needs?
4. Does it support staff needs and their wellbeing?

A child-centred philosophy needs to be geared towards a passion to achieve the best outcomes for children within a wellbeing driven environment providing mindfulness as a mechanism to enhance staff wellbeing and children's emotional intelligence.

Examples of philosophies:

■ Creating a generation of happy minds through child-centred play.

■ Mindful beings growing, flourishing one day at a time.

■ Creating joy and wellbeing through calm and creative learning.

Write your setting philosophy examples here:

… ....

....

....

If the setting philosophy is focused solely on educational outcomes and does not align to your personal philosophy (of a more balanced approach incorporating mindfulness), it could be challenging to work in an environment predominantly geared towards children's attainment rather than also consider wellbeing, mental health and building friendships.

The effectiveness of the pedagogy also often depends on the commitment and understanding of the practitioners and teachers and their integrity to ensure that it is embedded into the core of their teaching and care of children. Therefore, the personal values and beliefs of practitioners and teachers must be aligned to the core aims of the pedagogy.

Neuroscience: Supporting the case for children's mental health

Neuroscience is the scientific study of the nervous system, which comprises of two key systems, the central nervous system (brain and spinal cord) and the peripheral nervous system. The early years of a child's life are an important and vital time for children's development, as this is when they are going from being almost dependent new-borns to developing many new skills to become independent, communicate and lead healthy lives (CDC, 2020).

The first three years of life are a critical period for children's early brain development, as this is the time that the brain develops connections in prefrontal circuits at its fastest rate in childhood (Azarian, 2016), and as emphasised by the Centre for Educational Neuroscience (2020) 'deprivation over those years will result in persistent deficits in cognitive, emotional and even physical health'.

As early years practitioners, it is important to be aware that 90% of a child's brain develops during the first three years of their life, therefore early interactions are crucial for early brain development. Essentially recognising that most learning happens in the first three years of life because of how fast the brain develops and grows, starting before birth and continuing into early childhood (CDC, 2020). Research from Harvard University has found that early experiences are likely to have as much impact on health as on school achievement.

Figure 2.2   **Baby sitting on leaves.**

At birth, the average baby's brain is about a quarter of the size of the average adult brain. It doubles in size in the first year and continues to grow about 80% of adult size by age 3 and 90%, nearly fully grown by the age of 5 (First Things First, 2023).

Early brain development

Understanding how a baby's brain develops rapidly in the first three years will enable you to further comprehend that as the brain grows and develops, it produces billions of cells that make infinite neural connections, hard-wiring the brain through daily experiences in their environment.

These connections are crucial for children as they make developmental progress (child development) with opportunities for play-based repeated positive experiences in their daily routine. These interactions and engagement by parents, carers, EYPs and EYTs contribute to the learning and development of the brain. Therefore, planning activities and experiences such as singing, outdoor play, exploration, role play, daily conversations and games such as peek-a-boo, filling containers, sorting shapes, exploring a range of objects and materials ultimately support early brain development and children's emotional wellbeing.

Figure 2.3 **Pink brain with dumbbells wearing glasses.**

Alongside early brain development, there is increasing knowledge about emotions and their impact and role in children's learning and development. 'Children grow and learn best in a safe environment where they are protected from neglect and from extreme or chronic stress, with plenty of opportunities to play and explore' (CDC, 2020).

Exposure to stress and trauma can have long-term negative consequences for children's brains as identified in a study published by the Psychiatric Times in 2016. This study identified the prevalence of suicide attempts being higher in adults experiencing trauma, abuse and domestic violence as a child, and that is why practices such as mindfulness are increasingly being incorporated into classrooms and educational settings.

Azarian (2016) identifies that 'fundamental principles of neuroscience suggest that meditation can have its greatest impact on cognition when the brain is in its earliest stages of development'. The reason for this is the extra plasticity that creates the potential for meditation to have a greater impact on executive functioning, such as improved attention and impulse control as identified during a study relating to understanding the effectiveness of an 8-week mindfulness training for children with ADHD, aged 8–12(Van der Oord et al., 2011).

Neuroplasticity

The term neuroplasticity is another growing area for research and is a vital aspect of brain health and development for EYPs and EYTs to understand if they are to effectively support wellbeing and promote children's physical and mental health.

During the Mindfulness Education Summit (2018), Richard Davidson (PhD) shared the notion that 'neuroplasticity is simply the idea that the brain can change in response to experience, or in response to training'. From understanding that our brains change in response to stimuli, there is a growing field about the mechanisms of plasticity more so today than 10–20 years ago. Davidson (2018) also identified that these insights have provided us with a framework for understanding how a simple mental practice, like mindfulness can 'actually lead to systematic changes in the brain', within these key areas shown below.

Neuroimaging studies suggest that the practice of mindfulness meditation reliably changes the structure and function of the brain to increase blood flow and density to areas associated with decision-making and rational thinking, emotion regulation, learning and memory, kindness and compassion, and decreased density in areas involved in anxiety, worry and impulsiveness' (Weare, 2012).

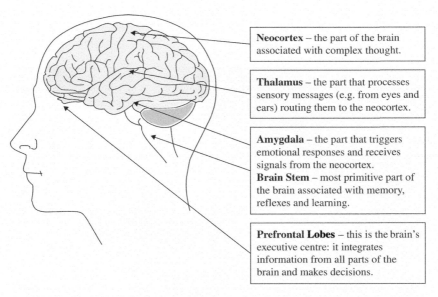

Figure 2.4 **Brain regions and functions.**

Rise in children's mental health

With a rising trend in child mental health from 1999 to the present time, including the worldwide pandemic of Covid-2019, the role of practitioners and teachers in promoting children's emotional wellbeing and positive mental health is more important than ever before. The 'Mental Health of Children and Young People in England 2017' survey (NHS Survey, 2017) identified some insight into the types of mental health problems experienced by pre-school children. The survey found that around 5.5% of pre-school children had at least one mental disorder; 2.5% had behavioural disorders; 1.4% with autism spectrum disorders and other common disorders related to sleeping and feeding; and more two- to four-year-old boys more likely to experience mental health problems than girls.

Research-based mindful pedagogy

Despite the limited research, EYPs and EYTs can aim to embed a pedagogy that provides a high-quality learning experience on the basis that a child's mental health is just as important as their physical health and equally important in preparing them for their future (Cache Website, 2020).

How well the brain develops depends on many factors in addition to genes including:

■ Good nutrition starting from pregnancy.

■ Exposure to toxins or infections.

■ The child's experiences with other people, their environment and the world.

The World Health Organization (WHO) recognise that this 'is the period of a child's life when the brain develops rapidly and the early foundations for health and

Figure 2.5 **Adult with baby looking at book.**

wellbeing are sown to support those important first few years of life and throughout their life' (WHO, 2019).

This emphasises the role of the adult in understanding the connection between early brain development and the impact on all areas of children's holistic development. How adults relate to children and provide play experiences in the early years, prepares them for school and later life by developing neural pathways within the brain, created from their experiences of the world. Therefore, adults including parents, carers, EYPs and EYTs need to provide the right care for children, starting before birth and continuing through childhood, to ensure that the brain grows well and reaches its full potential.

A study by Zeedyk (2012) informs us of one key insight into the development of the brain – that it is incomplete at birth due to the evolutionary process. The adult role is therefore fundamental in understanding that the growing brain is very flexible and adaptable at birth and develops externally within the environment that the baby finds him or herself.

Zeedyk (2012) also points out that the brain is developing more rapidly during the early years, particularly up to the age of three years, and that 'by age three approximately 90% of final brain mass is in place, with 70% in place by the age of one year'.

This research knowledge is vital for EYPs and EYTs to understand and to recognise how important the early years are and the role of the adult in developing those early nurturing relationships with babies.

This research informs us that babies can cope with a whole range of positive or negative situations within a range of different settings and environments, which ultimately form those early experiences.

Babies grow and develop through their learning and experiences, developing lasting neural pathways which (Cache Website, 2020) highlight is part of the preparation that helps children to have good mental health.

Although currently much of the focus and research tends to be about children of school age, children in their early years can be susceptible to poor mental health. An example of this relates to attachment issues that can affect babies and can escalate to more serious problems as children develop.

This was discussed by Mentally Healthy Schools (2021), who also recognise challenging behaviours, low mood, depression, anxiety, bereavement and eating problems as affecting mental health needs. Ashdown and Bernard (2012) further inform us that the early years of life are crucial in supporting the social and emotional development of babies, toddlers and pre-school children, recognised within one of the prime areas of learning in the EYFS, particularly the aspect, managing feelings and behaviour.

The limbic system

The basic architecture of the brain is constructed through an ongoing process that begins before birth and continues. Therefore, early experiences affect the quality of the architecture and establish the foundations for all learning, health and behaviour (developingchild.harvard.edu).

Research in the area of neuroscience also informs us of how children's thoughts and feelings are processed within the limbic system, the part of the brain where our moods, actions, emotions and memories are controlled.

A pedagogy with a mindful approach at its core encourages early years practitioners to interweave wellbeing aspects into daily practice with activities such as a feelings tree, daily conversations, belly breathing or a wonder walk supporting this area of the curriculum. 'Emotional wellbeing and social competence provide a strong foundation for emerging cognitive abilities. Therefore, the emotional and physical health, social skills and cognitive linguistic capacities that emerge in the early years are all important prerequisites for success in school' (developingchild.harvard.edu).

From these experiences, early years practitioners can use observation and evaluation processes to understand and empathise with children's behaviours and displayed emotions. It is important to recognise that the brain is most flexible or 'plastic' early in life to accommodate a range of environments and interactions. This early plasticity makes it easier and more effective to influence a baby's developing brain architecture that rewire it in later years. Daniel Siegel suggests that 'the power of mindfulness is to improve the physiology of both the teacher and the student' (Mindful Education Programme, 2018).

It is important for practitioners to be aware that when we practice mindfulness for ourselves and with children, we engage the cortex, which supports higher level thinking and how we react to situations. This part of the brain is also connected to speech, memories and how we consider and resolve problems. Therefore, early interactions with babies require stable, caring and interactive relationship building to benefit healthy brain development.

Case Study: Early Years Practitioner (EYP) in a Pre-School Setting

This case study explores the use of a range of mindfulness exercises and activities with children in one pre-school setting. As a practitioner my aim was to introduce a group of 3–4-year-old children and the staff team to a range of mindfulness activities over a period of four weeks.

The first step was to assess the outcomes through children's responses and the perceptions of the staff. The next step was to rationalise if mindfulness has the potential to be part of the daily curriculum and finally to evaluate the impact on children's wellbeing.

I was keen to find out if mindfulness supports the effects on children's wellbeing, particularly as some children are preparing for school and there is some degree of anxiety, worry and excitement.

Along with delivering the EYFS curriculum, we provide children with many sensory play experiences both indoors and outdoors in line with Montessori philosophy that sensory learning engages children's attention and absorbs their knowledge of the world through touch, smell, taste, sight and sounds.

The aim was to give the preschool children simple and short practices that supported their early life experiences and promoted their social, psychological, intellectual and emotional development using sensory interventions. I also wanted to introduce mindfulness activities to facilitate a smoother transition for the children who were moving towards more formal education.

Implementation of the mindfulness activities: The mindfulness sessions that I planned for the children were structured for three times a week over two weeks. There were six child-friendly sensory learning activities including a range of breathing exercises such as petal breathing and a soft toy placed on the children's tummy; a mindful glitter jar; a walk through the jungle; a range of mindful snack and mealtimes; mindful rope walking and listening to the sounds of musical instruments.

These activities relate to the EYFS characteristic of effective learning, playing and exploring which guides early years practitioners to encourage children to 'have a go' and experience new things DfE (2021).

Impact of mindfulness: For greater effectiveness and understanding, I incorporated a mindfulness session for staff and provided them with a handout showing various exercises that they could practice for themselves and with children. The outcomes were positive overall and there is now a better understanding of the benefits for children and staff involvement has increased.

Conclusion

This chapter introduced the concept of a mindful pedagogy and how this can be created and adapted as an approach in your early years setting. The terms mindfulness and pedagogy were carefully explored and links to theory underpinned their relevance to early years practice today. The chapter identified strategies and provided examples of how to develop a mindful pedagogy in your setting with a framework to support this implementation.

The importance of a child-centred approach to the pedagogy and philosophy was highlighted, with evidence for developing a setting wide awareness of the value of a mindful approach and how it impacts positively on children's individual needs and wellbeing. Understanding of supporting early brain development and the key role of the limbic system in supporting learning, behaviour and emotion regulation was discussed. Consideration of the Unique Child principle underpinned the chapter in defining your pedagogy in promoting happiness, calm and good mental health. The strategies and ideas within this chapter will enable you to explore a range of approaches and create a mindful pedagogy in your setting. It is important to retain that a mindful approach cannot be taught to children, it can only be modelled and guided by practitioners who understand the positive effects on a child's mental health.

References

Arnerich, M. (2021) *What is Pedagogy in the Early Years?* Accessed on 24 February 2021 at https://www.famly.co/blog/early-years-pedagogy

Ashdown, D. and Bernard, M. (2012) *Can Explicit Instruction in Social and Emotional Learning Skills Benefit the Social-Emotional Development, Well-being, and Academic Achievement of Young Children?* Accessed on 8 May 2021 at https://www.youcandoiteducation.com.au/wp-content/uploads/2020/01/Bernard-Impact-of-YCDI-Early-Childhood.pdf

Azarian, B. (2016) *The Mindful Child.* Accessed on 6 May 2021 at https://archive.nytimes.com/well.blogs.nytimes.com/2016/05/10/the-mindful-child/

Centre for Educational Neuroscience (2020) *Most Learning Happens in the First 3 Years.* Accessed on 3 July 2022 at http://www.educationalneuroscience.org.uk/resources/neuromyth-or-neurofact/most-learning-happens-in-the-first-3-years/

Centers for Disease Control and Prevention (CDC) (2020) *Early Brain Development and Health.* Accessed on 25 January 2022 at https://www.cdc.gov/ncbddd/childdevelopment/early-brain-development.html#:~:text=Children%20grow%20and%20learn%20best,and%20caring%20for%20their%20child

Cache Website (2020) *Mental Health During the Early Years.* Accessed on 30 January 2021 at https://www.cache.org.uk/news-media/mental-health-during-the-early-years

Child Mind Institute (2020a) *Children's Mental Health Report: Telehealth in an Increasingly Virtual World.* Accessed on 20 June 2021 at https://childmind.org/awareness-campaigns/childrens-mental-health-report/2020-childrens-mental-health-report/

Child Mind Institute (2020b) *How Can We Help Kids With Self-Regulation?* Accessed on 20 June 2021 at https://childmind.org/article/can-help-kids-self-regulation/

Davidson, R. (2018) *Neuroscience of Neuroplasticity.* (Online). Mindful Education Summit. Accessed on 18 June 2020. https://www.theawakenetwork.com/my-library/bonus-series/7-day-mindful-living-series/

Department for Education (DfE) (2012) *Statutory Framework for the Early Years Foundation Stage: Setting the Standards for Learning, Development and Care for Children from Birth to Five.* Accessed on 7 May 2021 at https://dera.ioe.ac.uk/id/eprint/14041/1/eyfs%20statutory%20framework%20march%202012.pdf

Department for Education (DfE) (2015) *Effective Pre-school, Primary and Secondary Education Project (EPPSE 3-16+).* Accessed on 5 April 2021 at https://www.ucl.ac.uk/ioe/sites/ioe/files/rb455_effective_pre-school_primary_and_secondary_education_project.pdf

Department for Education (DfE) (2020) *Development Matters: Non-statutory Curriculum Guidance for the Early Years Foundation Stage.* Accessed on 17 March 2021 at https://assets.publishing.service.gov.uk/government/uploads/system/uploads/attachment_data/file/1007446/6.7534_DfE_Development_Matters_Report_and_illustrations_web__2_.pdf

DfE Research Brief (2015) *Pedagogy in Early Childhood Education and Care (ECEC): An International Comparative Study of Approaches and Policies Research Brief.* Accessed on 15 October 2021 at https://assets.publishing.service.gov.uk/government/uploads/system/uploads/attachment_data/file/445817/RB400_-_Early_years_pedagogy_and_policy_an_international_study.pdf

First Things First (2023) *Brain Development.* Accessed on 28 February 2023 at https://www.firstthingsfirst.org/early-childhood-matters/brain-development/

Hawn, G. (2023) *Creating Healthier Minds for a Healthier World.* Accessed on 14 June 2023 at https://mindup.org/our-mission/

Johnson, J. (2014) *Becoming an Early Years Teacher, Chapter 2: The Early Years Teacher Role*: Citing Papatheodorou and Potts (2013), McGraw Hill Education. London.

Kabat-Zinn, J. (1990) *Full Catastrophe Living: Using the Wisdom of Your Mind and Body to Face Stress, Pain, and Illness.* London: Piatkus.

Mentally Healthy Schools (2021) Accessed on 4 December 2021, Available at https://www.mentallyhealthyschools.org.uk/mental-helth-needs/attachment-and-child-development/

Moriarty, S. (2018) *Wellbeing for Children in the EYFS.* Accessed on 19 December 2020 at https://www.cache.org.uk

Moyles, J., Adams, S. and Musgrove, A. (2002) *Early Years Practitioners' Understanding of Pedagogical Effectiveness: Defining and Managing Effective Pedagogy.* Accessed on 12 June 2021 at https://doi.org/10.1080/03004270285200291

Mukadam, Y. and Kaur, K. (2016) *The Early Years Handbook for Students and Practitioners.* Edited by Lyn Trodd, Oxon: Routledge.

National Health Service (NHS) Survey (2017) *Mental Health of Children and Young People in England, 2017; Summary of Key Findings.* Accessed on 11 January 2021 at https://files.digital.nhs.uk/A6/EA7D58/MHCYP%202017%20Summary.pdf

National Scientific Council on the Developing Child (2020) *Harvard University, Connecting the Brain to the Rest of the Body: Early Childhood Development and Lifelong Health Are Deeply Intertwined Working Paper No. 15.* Accessed on 19 January 2021 at https://developingchild.harvard.edu/

Nutbrown, C., Clough, P. and Selbie, P. (2008) *Early Childhood Education: History, Philosophy and Experience.* Sage: London.

Rouse, E. (2020) *Partnerships in the Early Years: Building Connections and Supporting Families.* Oxford University Press: Australia and New Zealand.

Siraj-Blatchford (2002) *Cited in Department for Education (DfE) OECD (2015). Pedagogy in early childhood education and care (ECEC): An International Comparative Study of Approaches and Policies.*

Standards and Testing Agency (2014) *Early Years foundation Stage Profile: Handbook.* [Online]. Accessed on 15 June 2021. https://www.gov.uk/government/publications/early-years-foundation-stage-profile-handbook

Taggart, G (2015) 'Sustaining Care: Cultivating Mindful Practice in Early Years Professional Development', *Early Years*, 35(4), pp. 381–393.

The Children's Society (2018) Accessed on 10 June 2020 at https://www.childrenssociety.org.uk

Van der Oord, S. et al. (2011) 'The Effectiveness of Mindfulness Training for Children With ADHD and Mindful Parenting for Their Parents', *Journal of Child and Family Studies*, 21, pp. 139–147.

Veale, F. (2016) *Early Years for Levels 4 & 5 and the Foundation Degree*. Oxon: Hodder Education.

Weare, K. (2012) *Evidence for the Impact of Mindfulness on Children and Young People (The Mindfulness in Schools Project Report)*. Accessed on 24 September 2021 at https://mindfulnessinschools. org/wp-content/uploads/2013/02/MiSP-Research-Summary-2012.pdf

World Health Organization (WHO) (2019) Accessed on 5 June 2021 at https://www.who. int/maternal_child_adolescent/topics/child/development/en/

Zeedyk, S. (2012) *'Babies' Brains Are Built On Connection …' The Science of Human Connection*. Accessed on 3 April 2021 at https://www.suzannezeedyk.com/wp-content/uploads/ 2016/03/Suzanne-Zeedyk-Human-brains-v3.pdf

3 Developing mindful environments in early years

Aims of Chapter 3

This chapter aims to:

■ Understand what constitutes a mindful learning environment.
■ Audit and review the existing learning environment for children.
■ Plan and organise a mindful learning environment led by children.
■ Create an early year's setting that supports children's emotional wellbeing.

Introduction

This chapter aims to introduce early years practitioners (EYPs) to the importance of developing the indoor and outdoor environment so that children have the ability to bond with the natural world and make the most of the experiences on offer. It is essential that all children can enjoy what is on offer within an inclusive, welcoming and accessible environment.

A range of strategies will be introduced that can be adopted to enable a sense of calmness and self-expression during the daily routine, instilling moments for children and practitioners to experience present-moment awareness and build inner peace and quietness of the mind. The focus is to create an emotionally literate environment that feels safe and secure. A key emphasis of this chapter is to review the current environment and to involve children in creating spaces that are easily accessible, which they feel belong to them rather than the staff.

DOI: 10.4324/9780429030734-4

The learning environment

The environment plays a key role in supporting and extending children's development and thinking. It is important to create a learning environment that:

■ Meets the needs of all children, their cultures and communities.

■ Offers stimulating resources and rich learning opportunities.

■ Provides a happy, safe and friendly place where children gain confidence in developing skills, taking risks and exploring.

■ Upholds a strong partnership between staff, parents and carers, who sensitively guide, value and support the individual care and learning of children.

Guidance by the DCSF (2008, p. 6) emphasises that children experiencing 'high quality early years provision are well placed to achieve better outcomes in school and beyond, and develop better social, emotional and cognitive abilities necessary for life-long learning'. Following this, the revised early years foundation stage (EYFS) (2012) gave practitioners, managers and professionals the opportunity to reflect upon current systems, routines and daily practice, highlighting the importance of the learning environment. A review by the Foundation Years (2012) identified that:

> In deciding what is an 'appropriate environment' it is important to understand the way babies, toddlers and young children learn and to provide for the age and stage of the children concerned. There is no ideal environment as babies' and young children's interests change, and the environment should be flexible to change in response to these changing interests.

This affirms our understanding that in early years, a rich and varied environment that meets the individual needs of children supports their learning and development. It gives them the confidence to explore and learn in secure and safe, yet challenging, indoor and outdoor spaces. The environment is made up of more than the physical space. In order for an early year setting to be a happy and welcoming environment, careful preparation of both the *physical and the emotional* environment is required for successfully supporting children's holistic development including emotional well-being. One of the elements identified by the DCSF (2008) guidance for quality improvement in early years is:

> Securing high quality environments for learning and development by focusing on the enabling environment (including the physical and emotional environment), which promotes children's well-being, nurtures children, and fosters positive relationships between children, parents and adults, and where children are valued for their uniqueness and individuality.

The emotional environment is an invisible measure of feelings experienced by the children, staff and parents that can be either positive or negative. Therefore, when planning the mindful learning environment, the aim is to ensure 'children feel safe and can express their feelings safely, knowing that staff are nearby to help them if they feel overwhelmed' (Early Years Matters, 2017). Teaching children to express their feelings allows them to externalise them safely to resolve problems as they arise, rather than prolonged stress or dissociation.

The role of the adult is crucial in developing a mindful learning environment that is emotionally supportive towards children's wellbeing. Therefore, as you work through this chapter to review and audit the existing learning environment, think about how to plan more purposeful and fluid spaces where adults are sensitive to the emotional needs of children, as well as fully present in implementing a fun, natural, calming and creatively resourced layout that meets the individual developmental needs of all children.

Strategies to support self-regulation in the learning environment

Self-regulation is defined by Dr Stuart Shanker (2020) as how children manage energy expenditure in response to daily stressors and then recover from the effort. He also emphasises that 'babies are all, in a fundamental sense, born premature', and the burst of neural growth and sculpting that takes place in the first year of life is when a baby's capacity for self-regulation and their 'stress-reactivity' is being wired, and once set, these trajectories can be difficult to change later in life.

Shanker (2020) identifies that in early years, the environment is one of the most common stressors for children, for example, too much noise, lighting or crowding. He identifies that self-regulation exists in five domains, each with its own range of stressors. The five interconnected domains of stressors are:

- Biological

- Emotional

- Cognitive

- Social

- Pro-social

Heightened stress in any or all these domains leads to negative downstream consequences. Therefore, as professionals working with children, we need to recognise that during this time of growth and development, adults play a critical role in observing and supporting children to manage daily stressors by learning the skill of how to self-regulate.

Therefore, when evaluating the daily environment and experiences in your setting, consider Shanker's (2020) guidance, which states that 'anyone concerned with the healthy development of a young child needs to pay close attention to the child's self-regulation, helping them feel safe and secure, and calming them when startled'.

It is also important to consider both the existing and revised environment consistently, observing children and recognising effective ways to support them to manage daily environmental and personal stressors that they may be experiencing. Stressors can vary significantly from one child to another and one moment to another, depending on their current physical and emotional state.

Self-regulation and the five domains of stressors are a crucial aspect to reflect upon when developing a mindful learning environment, not only for our own self-regulation practice but also when supporting children to self-regulate and practice this essential skill, with the aim towards doing so independently. Shanker (2020) identifies that with adult support children can learn to identify and reduce stressors as a first step towards easing their stress levels and bringing them back to a calm and focused state more quickly, ultimately improving their ability to self-regulate.

This framework provides a foundation to creating an effective mindful learning environment, which enables reflection and understanding of supporting children's emotional health. It also sets expectations of adults to provide an environment where warmth and inclusivity is valued and where all genders, cultures, abilities, special educational needs and disabilities are embraced.

Scaffolding and modelling by adults validate the view that a good emotional environment will 'provide a secure base from which children grow into well-rounded, capable adults with robust mental health' (DfE, 2009).

Biological
- Being hungry or thirsty, poor sleeping habits, excessive visual stimulation, insufficient exercise, sitting still too long, uncomfortable clothing, smells and cluttered spaces.

Emotional
- Changes to the daily routine, a new key person, issues at home affecting emotional state, peer pressure, tiredness, transitions at home or in the setting causing intense emotions relating to divorce, moving home, a new baby, grief or loss.

Cognitive
- Learning something new, boredom, organising thoughts, challenging tasks, following a set of instructions, understanding a new concept or skill e.g. counting, measuring and time.

Social
- Difficulty picking up on social cues or understanding the effect of their behaviour on others, being left out, bullied, crowded classroom/setting, feeling shy, jealous, making friends

Proscoial
- Difficulty coping with other people's stress, a baby crying, an upset peer, not understanding sharing, guilt, illness in the family, empathy/ sympathy, understanding right or wrong.

Figure 3.1 **Diagram illustrating the five domains of stressors (adapted from The MEHRIT Centre Toolkit, 2017).**

Activity

Consider the range of stressors identified in Figure 3.1, then:

a. Reflect on your current provision and identify some of the existing stressors children may be experiencing.

b. Complete Table 3.1 with some of the key stressors with proposed changes in creating a more mindful learning environment to reduce these stressors.

Supporting enabling and mindful environments

A rich and varied environment supports children's emotional learning and development as it gives them the confidence to interact with others, learn key skills in self-regulation modelled by adults and builds their capacity to manage stressors within a safe, secure space supported by understanding and caring adults.

The EYFS identifies the importance of providing experiences for children within an indoor and outdoor environment with the Early Years Alliance (2019) suggesting that the environment offers activities for indoor and outdoor play, with sufficient space for children to explore, move, collaborate and risk take.

Table 3.1   **Table of Stressors and Proposed Changes to Enhance the Mindful Early Years Environment**

Domain	Existing stressors	Changes to create a more mindful environment
Biological		
Emotional		
Cognitive		
Social		
Prosocial		

Tina Bruce (2011) articulates one of Froebel's principles that 'quality education is about three things: the child, *the context in which the learning takes place* and the knowledge and understanding that the child develops and learns'.

In addition, Maria Montessori believed that the role of education is to provide environments in which the children can be set free to follow their natural impulses and to become the wonderfully dynamic, natural learners they are designed to be.

As we know, there is no such thing as a typical learning environment in early years. This is dependent upon several factors including:

■ The children, their individual needs and interests

■ The physical layout of the indoor and outdoor spaces

■ The size of the setting and the resources

■ The creativity and vision of ALL adults working at the setting

Therefore, to even start to contemplate how to develop a **mindful environment** within your early years setting, it is important to firstly consider the above and these two key areas:

■ The statutory requirements of the EYFS and its guiding principles

■ If your setting has a 'culture' of mindfulness or potential to develop one

The latter is highly important because *if the staff team do not fully hold the concepts of mindfulness in high regards*, or they do not understand the value of developing a mindful environment, then the benefits will always remain limited for the children.

One of the overarching principles of the EYFS to shape practice in early years settings is that 'Children learn and develop well in enabling environments, in which their experiences respond to their individual needs and there is strong partnership between practitioners and parents and carers'. (DfE, 2017, p. 6). Therefore, planning a playful and purposeful learning environment is a key responsibility of an early year's team and the ongoing process is fundamental in enabling individuals and teams to reflect upon practice, review the existing learning environment and develop it accordingly to support children's interests, care and education.

Before embarking on a journey of creating spaces and opportunities that support wellbeing, calmness and mindful moments for children, it is important to reflect on the current environment. To gain a holistic perspective of the *current* learning environment, we can apply **Brookfield's Lenses** to consider and evaluate what to offer from the *lens of a child, the adults, the self and the literature including the EYFS.*

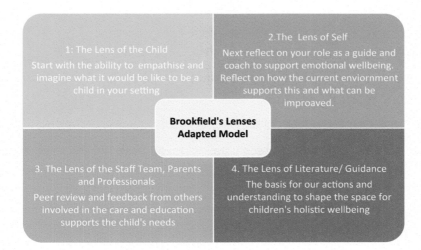

Figure 3.2   **Brookfield's (1995) adapted reflection model.**

Drawing upon each of the four lenses (perspectives) is a good starting point to reflect upon your current setting environment.

Staff activity

Critical reflection of the current setting environment.

The questions in this reflective activity will enable you to objectively review the existing learning environment, applying the adapted Brookfield's Lenses model to successfully audit the physical and emotional environments, indoors and outdoors.

Audit Questions:

1. First, identify three positive features of the current learning environment in your setting that support calm and restful practices and adult interactions for emotional support.

2. How well is the current environment set up, resourced and arranged for the children?

3. What is in place to welcome children and visitors?

4. Are the indoor and outdoor areas currently integrated to support free flow for child-initiated play, exploration and self-expression?

5. Are there opportunities for developing warm caring relationships and expression of feelings, essential to children's' wellbeing?

6. What is the role of adults during the daily routine to support children's emotional health?

7. What is your current understanding of an emotional learning environment?

8. What daily activities or techniques do you have in place to support children's emotional wellbeing?

Notes:..

....

....

....

Developing a mindful learning environment

In practice, a mindful learning environment aligns with and is made up of specific components that liken to the 'emotional learning environment'. 'An emotional learning environment is one that promotes wellbeing and provides stability for children according to their individual needs' (Strong-Wilson and Ellis, 2007).

In essence, this definition highlights that a robust emotionally literate environment shapes the 'mindful environment' as it is centred upon the requisites of the emotional environment and includes a range of mindfulness activities and techniques that support children's wellbeing.

The two terms 'mindful' and 'emotional' can be used interchangeably; however, for the purposes of this book, we will continue to focus on the term 'mindful', which does not replace the term emotional, rather clarifies its purpose for early years teachers (EYTs) and EYPs when promoting routines and approaches to enhancing children's wellbeing.

The adult plays a fundamental role in promoting an inclusive environment where all children are valued for their uniqueness regardless of gender, religion, ethnicity, background, languages spoken, special educational needs or disabilities. A determined effort to adapt and support daily routines and learning opportunities for children with less emphasis on their own ideas of what children need, but to consider the environment and the curriculum first and foremost from the child's perspective with and understanding of their feelings.

This, in turn, will support the emotional wellbeing of children in daily situations to develop foundational skills such as *self-regulation, resilience, independence, managing daily stressors, recognising and understanding their feelings and* emotions.

Froebel based much of his understanding of children by observing them. He believed that children construct their understanding of the world through direct experience with it (Bruce, 2011). Therefore, it is important for EYPs and EYTs to create the environment both indoors and outdoors by observing children and consider a Froebelian principled approach, particularly that the 'practitioner must nurture the ideas, feelings, relationships and physical development and embodiment of children'. This approach is similar to a mindful approach in that practitioners create a warm affectionate atmosphere that opens children up to learning and supports them to know themselves, respect themselves and engage with their learning positively (Department for Education (DfE), 2020).

Being guided by adults within an environment electing to adopt a predominant **relational approach** as central to nurturing children's positive behaviours and support the mindful emotion led environment. This will essentially 'provide a secure base from which children grow into well rounded, capable adults with robust mental health' (DfE, 2003).

The term 'mindful-centred environment' can be identified as:

■ A place where children's feelings and wellbeing are a priority.

■ A warm and welcoming environment where all children are accepted as individuals in their own right and treated fairly.

■ A safe place where adults promote emotional wellbeing and support children to express their feelings, without ignoring, making judgments or criticising.

■ A mindful learning environment where adults themselves are in the present moment, with real empathy and compassion for children as they transition through the daily routine.

■ Made up of spaces and areas for children to rest, have quiet time, stay calm with responsive adults to help them overcome any challenges they may face.

■ Good role models in adults where the focus is on providing emotional support and exploring thoughts, ideas and feelings appropriately with children, so they know that they will be accepted and understood by the adults around them.

■ A place where children support one another and learn about their own emotions, positive or negative.

Strategies for creating an effective mindful learning environment

Designing a quality mindful learning environment enables babies and children to express their emotions safely guided by supportive adults with a consistent approach and understanding of children's emotional learning and how to support them to understand how to express, regulate and respond to daily stressors and develop those prime area skills within the daily routines and experiences.

Here are some strategies to consider for creating your **mindful-centred (emotional) learning** environment. Some of these ideas are drawn from the book Supporting Toddlers' Wellbeing in Early Years Settings: Strategies and Tools for Practitioners and Teachers (Mukadam and Sutherland, 2018).

1. Create a rich and stimulating child-centred environment that encourages a sense of belonging for children, so that they feel at ease with their surroundings.

2. A home from home environment where their emotions are accepted and understood by caring and sensitive adults who respect each child's unique interests.

3. Awareness of children's facial expressions, body language, verbal cues and physical interactions so that they feel supported to express their feelings within a safe and nurturing environment.

4. Working in a team to effectively review and plan the space regularly to maintain the mindful environment that promotes use of quiet spaces, with opportunities for children to rest, work quietly, get creative or imaginative during their play.

5. Adults to interact and co-regulate to support children to manage feelings and emotions as they form friendships, manage challenges, share and make choices in their learning environment.

6. Review the equipment, furniture and resources and how these can be best organised indoors and outdoors including children and families to contribute their ideas to develop a sense of ownership and more purpose to the play experience.

7. Lastly, consider the fundamental responsibility of keeping children safe when planning the setting environment and supporting play and learning. Take into account risks and hazards both indoors and outdoors and support children to manage risk and gain confidence in their skills and abilities.

Interventions to assess wellbeing within daily practice will underpin an overarching wellbeing philosophy using audit tools to assess wellbeing when reviewing the effectiveness of the environment such as:

a. Sustained Shared Thinking and Emotional Wellbeing (SSTEW) (Siraj et al., 2015)

b. Leuven Wellbeing and Involvement Scales (Laevers, 2005)

These strategies can be adapted to support a range of setting environments and are inclusive to children across the age ranges, with particular needs and interests. They will form the basis for a quality learning environment increasing wellbeing, confidence and involvement of children.

Designing the layout of your mindful-led emotional learning environment

A child–centred layout for your mindful learning environment can begin by reflecting upon some of the strategies listed above and by considering the four areas identified in the diagram below, representing your mindful learning environment.

1. **Physical space and resources:**
   Calming environment, labelled, safe, hazards identified. Natural resources and materials, natural environment, age–appropriate resources.

2. **Mindful practices:**
   Promoting wellbeing, mindful activities to build resilience, nurturing; calming spaces for quiet activities; supporting basic needs and personal, social and emotional (PSE) development.

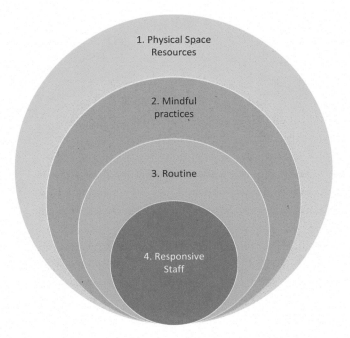

Figure 3.3 **Four-steps model of a mindful learning environment.**

3. **Routine**:

A consistent routine that children are familiar with, including quiet mindful activities after sleep, rest and mealtimes. Collaboration with children and families to support mindful approaches.

4. **Responsive staff:**

Leaders, managers and practitioners work together to guide, coach and support emotional learning, building trusting relationships.

This four-step process begins your plans to create the emotional environment, which enables an invisible measure of children's feelings, where practitioners, visitors, families and most importantly all children notice a 'feel good' factor when they are in the setting. Additionally, feeling safe in the physical and emotional environment will support children to express their feelings safely, knowing that knowledgeable and understanding practitioners are close by to support them if they feel overwhelmed or are experiencing stressors. This will ultimately help children to manage their emotions and resolve feelings that are impacting on their wellbeing.

How the emotional environment supports learning and development

The EYFS identifies a child's social and emotional development as one of the prime areas of learning and development. If children are to achieve their full potential, their communication, social and emotional skills are vital for their future relationships, decisions and managing everyday situations.

Within a caring and nurturing environment, children will have a positive disposition to learning, sharing and working co-operatively, show empathy and have confidence to achieve their life and career goals (Table 3.2). They will also be equipped to manage transitions and challenging situations in their life, such as a new class, school, house move, family situation and exams. Many children are exposed to traumatic events in their early years of life. While many return to a normal state of functioning, *if the trauma is ongoing this can have an impact on their long-term health*. A study relating to childhood trauma, published in 2015, showed that the more adverse childhood experiences a person has, the higher their risk of health problems later in life.

It is important that different cultures, religions and languages reflected within the setting welcome diversity and respect the values and beliefs of all children and their uniqueness. This can include welcome signs in all languages representing the families attending, family photographs of celebrations, books in different languages and depicting a range of characters. Images that reflect the diversity of children, families and staff and resources and activities reflecting children's interests and cultures.

Table 3.2   **Table of Strategies in Creating a Positive Emotional Environment for Children**

Key component	Description	How can this be achieved
A home from home environment	Personalise the setting to make children and families feel valued. Children like familiar things and this helps them feel a sense of ownership and belonging. touch as much as possible.	■ Use their name ■ Warm welcome to child and family (this will have a positive impact on everyone) ■ Inclusive and familiar activities, e.g. hello song and morning yoga ■ Share news and items from home ■ Family photographs on a display ■ Plan activities children want to do, engage families
Build Positive Relationships	Children require time to settle into an unfamiliar environment. Give them time to form bonds of attachment, rather than allocate a child to a key person. Strong bonds are enabled by developing regular communication with the family, understanding the child's needs and what helps them to settle and feel happy, calm and relaxed.	■ Daily observations to understand children's needs ■ Active listening to supporting emotional wellbeing ■ Activities to support emotional literacy, e.g. movement to music, sensory area to relax ■ Develop communication with the family
Personal choice	Enable children to make choices about their environment. This supports them to analyse and make decisions, a key skill through childhood and in later life. The environment needs to be geared towards their choices rather than the adults' perceptions.	■ Encourage the child to choose activities and resources ■ Give them time to explore ■ Plan areas of the environment where children choose what they would like to do
Routine and consistency	Establishing a daily routine sets boundaries for children and consistency in their day. Flexibility within this supports emotional needs being met and planning the emotional environment can support managing behaviour.	■ Show or explain the routine to children ■ Talk through what they can choose to do and await their responses ■ Provide choices within the routine to develop decision making

(Continued)

Table 3.2   Table of Strategies in Creating a Positive Emotional Environment for Children (*Continued*)

Key component	Description	How can this be achieved
Celebrate achievements and efforts to build self-esteem and confidence	The daily routine and environment should make time to celebrate what children have achieved and the efforts they have made. This gives them confidence when they attempt future activities and experiences.	■ Display children's work with their name and age ■ Share achievements and milestones with families and other children ■ Use positive words and praise ■ Present certificates and recognise positive behaviours at circle time
Managing emotions and feelings	Model calm and compassion when supporting children to manage their feelings. Help children understand 'rules' and 'boundaries'.	■ If conflicts arise, speak adapting the tone of voice to suit the situation ■ Co-regulate to support self-regulation ■ Identify strategies to support children to manage feelings
Independence	Ultimately work towards supporting independence and developing skills physically, emotionally and mentally.	■ Visual and verbal reminders for handwashing and toileting ■ Provide resources and activities to support emotional and mental wellbeing, e.g. story time, singing, drawing and open-ended activities

Audit of the existing physical and emotional early years environment

Auditing the existing environments enable EYPs and EYTs to identify key features and limitations within the setting. Many staff spend a considerable amount of time each day, week, month and year to plan and ensure that the learning environment, both indoors and outdoors, meets children's developmental needs.

For an effective child–centred mindful learning environment, it is important to start from the child's perspective. This aligns with current early years practice that is influenced by Froebel's philosophy, which begins with the observation of the child, enabling adults to tune in and support the learning. Froebel believed that each child is a unique individual and makes connections to their learning in their own way (Bruce, 2011). This is a reminder to practitioners to look beyond the statutory requirements of Ofsted and the EYFS to fully experience the environment as a physical ever-changing space and an emotionally safe and nurturing place to inspire and develop children's creativity and emotional wellbeing.

Reflection: Why do you think it is important to establish a 'mindful culture' in preparation for a mindful learning environment?

....

....

....

Here is an outline of the three steps required in creating your mindful learning environment and culture:

■ **Step 1:** Scope the physical and emotional environment both indoors and outdoors, auditing the space, layout and resources available and how these can be enhanced and contribute towards developing a wellbeing curriculum. Consider what children have to say within this aspect.

■ **Step 2:** Identify the role of the adults and their responsibilities to nurture and create an environment that values and respects the individual needs of the children.

■ **Step 3:** Plan a layout, daily routine and design that all staff and children have contributed to. Create an aesthetically pleasing indoor and outdoor space to heighten children's experiences and appreciation of the natural world, and experiences that support their learning, emotional wellbeing and holistic development, care and learning.

Activity

You will now analyse your early years environment in more detail.

Step 1:

Start by scoping the current physical and emotional environment both indoors and outdoors, considering your response to the previous reflective activity.

Next complete the **audit tool (Table 3.3) to identify the level of mindfulness practices in place** rating each area 1 to 5 (where 1 is low level and 5 is high level of mindfulness practice).

Key for rating mindfulness:

1. Low level adult interaction with child and limited mindful activities and practices

2. Limited and inconsistent level of interactions to support wellbeing

3. Some level of consistency from some adults to support wellbeing

4. Consistent approach to mindfulness with interaction by most adults

5. Consistent approach across staff team to interact, plan and evaluate the environment; and co-regulate with children

Table 3.3 **Audit of the Current Physical and Emotional Environment**

Mindful indoor environment	Yes/no/ never/ sometimes	Mindfulness rating level scale: 1 to 5	Areas to develop
Is the indoor environment inviting, well-ventilated and a friendly place to walk into			
Are children greeted and welcomed by all staff and is there a welcome display			
Is the layout safe with a range of activities and resources accessible at child height			
Are activities suitable for the age ranges and play based to encourage experiential play			
Does the layout invite self-care and self-expression, i.e. puppets, dolls, quiet spaces, soft lighting, sensory soft play, classical music and role play			
Are areas clearly defined and set up for children with word and picture labels			
Are there assigned areas for children to rest, sit and enjoy moments of calm and relax			
Does the daily routine include physical movement such as stretching, fitness, dance and yoga, to encourage growth and development			
Are there daily opportunities for mental health such as yoga, mindful walks, breathing practices, rest and listening to music			
Are there visual resources such as books, games and posters to promote talk about emotions and feelings			
Is the room layout organised to engage children to interact and promote their communication skills			
Are there group activities to support building relationships, playing co-operatively and sharing resources			
Do areas incorporate the characteristics of effective learning			
Are resources age/stage appropriate			

(Continued)

Table 3.3   **Audit of the Current Physical and Emotional Environment (*Continued*)**

Mindful indoor environment	*Yes/no/ never/ sometimes*	*Mindfulness rating level scale: 1 to 5*	*Areas to develop*
Mindful outdoor environment			
Do children have access to the outdoor area throughout the day			
Is the area well organised and inviting			
Does the space promote a child-centred environment			
Do activities and experiences outdoors complement (rather than duplicate) the indoor environment			
Do children have opportunities to investigate and explore the natural environment:			
Growing and planting			
Investigating mini beasts			
Seasonal changes			
Dens, camping and mindful walks			
Do children have the opportunity to explore natural materials:			
Forest school activities			
Mud kitchen			
Sand and water			
Collages, creative and imaginative play			
Are there relevant labels and signs around the environment			
Do the activities offer breadth across the areas of learning			
Is it a natural setting			
Is there a forest school space			

Source: Adapted from Northamptonshire County Council, Early Years Improvement Team Learning Environment Audit: A tool for settings, 2017.

Reflection: From the audit, identify how the current indoor and outdoor environment promote the emotional wellbeing of children and what level of mindfulness activity is evident within the setting routine. Summarise this in your own words below:

....

....

....

Step 2: Find time to *identify the responsibilities of the staff team to nurture and create an environment* that values and respects the individual needs of the children. EYPs and EYTs play a vital role in providing a purposeful space for children to flourish. Use this step to self-reflect on the key responsibilities of adults in providing an environment that respects and values *children's individual needs*, *their emotional wellbeing, resilience, confidence and self-esteem*. Evidence shows that regular mindfulness practices can achieve lower levels of stress and higher wellbeing scores. Supporting children's mental health, mindfulness enables children to do what they do best, which is to exist in the present moment. This is a vital life skill that adults support alongside self-regulation where children learn to manage their emotions and feelings. Additionally, parents play a vital role in their child's learning from birth, as research by Sammons et al. (2007) identifies how the home environment is the single biggest influence on a child's development in either a positive or negative way.

Activity

Reflective questions for EYPs and EYTs:

1. What are the key reasons that lead you to plan to make changes to the setting environment?

2. How do you ensure that these changes impact positively on children's experiences?

3. Why is it important to value and respect children's needs when planning any change?

4. How does the current setting environment enable children to express their emotions and feelings?

Points to consider when developing the mindful learning environment for each age group

The role of the staff team is to provide an enabling environment for children. It is essential that all staff understand how children learn (Oxfordshire County Council, 2008; Oxfordshire.gov.uk). In this case, it is essential that staff understand how to support their emotional wellbeing, by providing experiences and opportunities through play enabling resilience, calm, inner peace, compassion and self-esteem.

The toddler room/area

Create spaces that children can explore and can gain a sense of serenity when they enter. An indoor area can be set up using soft and neutral colours, low level displays, soothing music as children enter the setting with low level lighting to create a feeling of calmness and wellbeing. It is also important to consider the outdoor environment as an area that requires the same thought, planning and consideration of the spaces for children to explore and make sense of the world around them. This gives children the ability to bond with the natural world, experiencing a sense of freedom to venture beyond their known experiences with confidence and guidance from practitioners/ teachers. A range of strategies can be introduced that can be adopted to enable a sense of calmness and self-expression during the daily routine, instilling moments for children and practitioners/teachers to experience present moment awareness and build inner peace and quietness of the mind.

Baby room/area

An open and airy environment with adequate space can be organised to suit the number of babies and their needs and interests on a day to day basis. A range of treasure baskets set out when children enter the setting will provide a range of natural materials for children to settle and explore, enhancing sensory play. A small area of grass indoors will provide a green natural surface for babies to sit, crawl and walk on, providing an outdoor experience.

Pre-school room/area

Children entering a mindful early year's environment will experience a range of carefully planned spaces that enable them to take up opportunities where they can express their thoughts and emotions within a safe and caring environment. This could include a wellbeing tree to share their feelings and thoughts throughout the day. Overall the role of the adult is to interweave a range of spaces that engage and settle children's emotions and feelings. When entering a setting, the experiences from home impact on children's moods. Introduce quiet areas, cosy areas such as dens, reading and music spaces for children to access safely, with adults facilitating quiet time and modelling this appropriately.

The early years is a fundamental time to support children developing emotional wellbeing and self-regulation skills, and the mindful learning environment will enable practitioners to support children and work with them in creating spaces suitable and consistent to their needs.

Step 3: This is the planning stage of your child-centred environment and is an opportunity to create an aesthetically pleasing space indoors and outdoors to heighten children's experiences and appreciation of the beautiful world around them.

The building blocks to creating the 'mindful learning environment' is taking shape *with the audit completed and areas to focus on identified*.

Planning the mindful environment

An effective way to plan the mindful environment is to use this **'Mindful Spaces 3-s Step Plan'**. This will enable you to assess and design a mindful learning environment which considers the child at the centre of the process.

This will be an effective tool for practitioners/teachers to use when checking the wellbeing of children and to determine if each space is supporting emotional engagement, physical wellbeing and mental wellbeing.

The model provides an effective mechanism to assess the current environment and its suitability in enhancing the emotional wellbeing of children using a three-layer approach. This will ensure that the physical space incorporates a range of play experiences that encourage self-regulation, confidence, independence and building early relationships such as a 'wellbeing garden'.

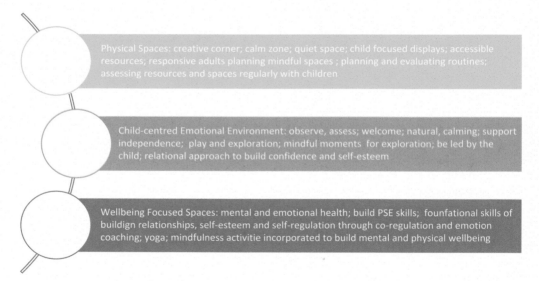

Figure 3.4 **Mindful spaces three-step plan.**

With the spaces and their criteria covered, the staff are now in a good position to model and support the development of behaviours and skills that are valued in society that children can start to build solid foundations from. For example, activities enhancing their ability to manage social situations (role play, puppet play), express their opinions and feelings without judgment or end products (clay, dough, junk modelling), and manage their emotions and connecting with their inner feelings within a safe and supportive environment with adults modelling compassion, empathy and listening to children.

Although adults spend a lot of their time planning and preparing the physical layout and resources for the environment, the emotional environment is often overlooked, and this aspect will enable you to put wellbeing at the heart of the early years' experience for children and their families.

Strategies to apply for developing the emotional environment

You may like to start by considering posters and displays that engage children's attention and emotions. For example, artefacts, objects, art and activities that spark interest, story boards, an art gallery to showcase children's learning, a yoga sequence to practice daily, a dance routine choreographed by the children, vocal expression through singing, poetry, rhyme and singing and dancing; poster of children doing yoga poses displayed; props such as puppets to tap into roles and empathy towards others.

Activity

Draw a plan of your mindful learning environment.
 Here are some points to consider when doing this activity:

■ When planning mindful spaces in your learning environment, provide areas for children to sit and be calm, express their feelings, manage stressors and use their voices within a safe and supportive environment.

■ The success of a mindful environment are mindful adults. Chapter 4 provides techniques and practices for staff wellbeing and mindful practices to enhance adults mindful state, mental health and overall wellbeing.

■ When considering the routine and organising the space, include opportunities for parents and carers to get involved and share their skills, e.g. a doctor talking about how the brain works is a fascinating activity for children which I set up in a nursery that I worked in. *This will* support children to learn about their brain, work with others, build relationships, share their emotions and interact in a positive and caring environment.

Plan for developing a mindful learning environment
Creating and implementing your mindful environment

From the information in this chapter and the activities complete, you are now better informed to create and implement your own mindful-centred learning environment.

The key criteria below are a checklist guide for you to refer to, as you begin the transformation process to creating the child-centred mindful environment at your setting:

- **Criteria 1:** The needs, interests and preferences of the child are central to the mindful environment, evidenced from observations, assessments and your interactions with the children and families.

- **Criteria 2:** Practices and routines need to be conducive to supporting emotion regulation, children's self-regulation and resilience with a range of spaces that enable group activities, time for children to sit on their own or in small groups to rest, feel calm, express their thoughts, ideas and feelings.

- **Criteria 3:** EYFS guidance and principles for early years learning environments must be understood and adhered to and consideration of your mindful pedagogical approach that you created in Chapter 2

Make some reflective notes here about the criteria above and how will this support you in creating your mindful learning environment:

....

....

....

Activity

You are now ready to design a layout for your whole setting environment in collaboration with the staff team and others involved in planning the learning environment.

Use A3 paper or create a digital plan scoping out your mindful learning environment. Consider the ideas discussed in this chapter and apply the cyclical process provided in Figure 3.5.

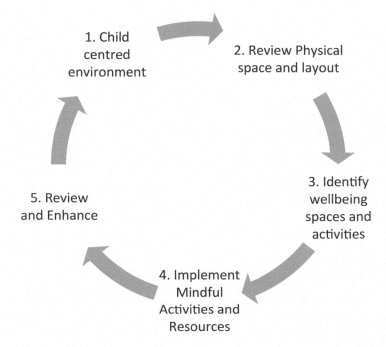

Figure 3.5 **Cyclical process for planning your mindful learning environment.**

Review and enhance the environment

Continued evaluation of the environment will enable new staff and existing staff to consider wellbeing from different perspectives, inviting fresh ideas and perceptions for exploration. Effective ways to maintain engagement and interactions with all staff include:

■ Review regularly at team meetings, a room meeting, daily chats, review observations, feedback from parents and visitors. Then evaluate the benefits to children and plan areas for development over a 6 week period. Also check if aspects of the Early Learning Goals (ELGs) are being met or supported, particularly the wellbeing aspects statements.

■ As a team continue to brainstorm and collate ideas about the layout, the space, the routine and roles. This requires collaboration and team working from start to finish. If only one person is on board, the changes will not be beneficial for children, the setting or you.

For a successful change to occur, build trusting relationships with children, parents, carers and colleagues at all times and keep everyone involved. Implementing a mindfulness programme as a trainer is different to what you are developing. You are introducing elements of mindfulness to support children to self-regulate, manage their feelings and to have opportunities to feel calm without overstimulation of activities, noise and too many challenges. By focusing on the prime areas will enable practitioners to develop a mindful learning environment without the concern of educational attainment as the priority.

Here are some reflective questions to support you to continually review and develop your mindful learning environment.

1. What is working well?

2. What could be changed and why?

3. What one thing can we do differently to support the development of the mindful learning environment?

4. How can we measure and share the impact of the mindful environment?

Case Study

Tiffany Murison: EYP, Forest School Leader and Early Years Graduate in Education and Leadership in Practice

Over the last 5 years of my career in early years, I have begun being more intentional about supporting children's wellbeing through the use of mindfulness. Finding ways to be fully present in the moment with the children, helping them tune into their physical and mental states and encouraging them to be aware of their thoughts and emotions has been the main focus of my practice.

It was important to me that adding mindfulness into teaching was not going to create 'extra work' given how much work EYPs already have on their plates. If I wanted to build a model that was sustainable for myself and others it had to be achievable.

Embedding in practice

The first thing anyone says when you talk about a new method is that they do not have time and cannot add to their workload. Being mindful does not have to be something extra that is added to an already heavy workload if it is embedded in your already existing systems and routines. One of the ways that I added mindfulness to my practice is by ensuring that our routine has enough time for us to move slowly through transitions as well as it being flexible enough that if the children are deeply involved then they do not need to be pulled away. By building room for the time needed to think, feel and connect, the children and staff do not feel hurried and their wellbeing is supported by being able to be in the moment.

Another benefit of not feeling rushed is that practitioners feel better able to engage with children during feelings of distress. The allowance of time means that practitioners can talk with children about what they are feeling without the need to distract them to move them on. The ability to examine their emotions helps children to learn to regulate them which, in the long run, can help them to be more present and aware of their thoughts and feelings.

A third method I used to embed mindfulness in daily routine was demonstrating to the children how to be in the moment, how to enjoy slowing down and that time engaging in these moments was valued. I firmly believe that showing a child that sitting and watching the wind blow the leaves in the trees is as valuable as practicing their writing will help build their foundation of wellbeing.

Activities

In addition to making mindfulness a part of our routine, I offered games and activities that would help the children to grasp the more intangible ideas of mindfulness such as controlling their breathing, physical grounding, awareness of their body's reaction to emotion and visualisation.

Games for breath control involved needing to blow harder or softer depending on the desired result. One that I found the children often enjoyed was blowing pom poms with a straw. We set up different challenges on the tables such as a line across one end of the table and the goal was to take a deep breath and blow the pom pom across the line in one try. Another challenge that was aimed at teaching the children to blow softly was a maze that they had to blow the pom pom around. If they blew too hard, the pom pom tended to bounce out of the track, so they had to be careful and in control.

To help the children learn to visualise, we would sit in small groups and tell stories. As the children told their stories, the practitioner would ask questions about how things looked, smelled or sounded, which would support them to practise visualising while in a calm and safe moment.

Grounding is a method of mindfulness that is sometimes used to help someone when they are feeling anxious or fearful, and it was included in all of our forest school sessions. It helps the individual focus and become more present by bringing their attention to physical sensations such as the ground under their feet, the pressure of a touch or the wind blowing on their skin. Spending time drawing the children's attention to these types of things in a playful way helps them to be able to practise this method when they feel upset. We used forest school sessions to give the children time to explore their environment and their relationships with each other in a mindful way. We talked about being present and aware of what was on the outside of their body as well as on the inside. By asking them to consider what sensory experiences they were having as well as what they were thinking and feeling we helped them to learn to be present in each moment.

The children

During the last couple of years, I worked with a few children, at different nurseries, who struggled with anxiety more than is typical for their ages. By incorporating various mindfulness strategies, the children learned to communicate about, and regulate, their strong feelings.

One child in particular stands out because she experienced anxiety and panic attacks almost daily. As a team we worked closely with her parents in an effort to determine if there was a consistent cause and it appeared to be a lack of confidence leading to her feeling unsure and therefor unsafe. I proposed to her family that we could use mindfulness techniques to support her when she was feeling anxious, so that we could help her work through her fear, and they agreed. Together we developed a plan of activities and techniques to teach her ways to calm down when she was overwhelmed so that she could face her fears without feeling panicked. We provided her with a few different strategies, such as breath control, visualisations and body awareness. She most preferred to use the breath control techniques and after a short while was able to initiate these strategies on her own. After approximately six months, she was more aware of her body and could communicate when she was beginning to feel scared and would immediately start using her mindfulness strategies to calm her thoughts. She began to exhibit more confidence in the areas that used to frighten her and was observably happier; within a year she no longer had anxiety attacks at all.

Adding mindfulness to your practice is invaluable, for practitioners and the children, but does require a commitment from everyone involved because, like anything new, the key is to be consistent. After years of using mindfulness, it has become simply a part of how I teach, and I am incredibly grateful to have a way to support and improve the wellbeing of the children in my care.

Conclusion

A mindful environment is one that is purposefully planned to provide a calming, interesting, natural, safe and rich enabling space in which children can play, explore and learn. This type of environment can contribute greatly to a mindful culture to support children's emotional health within a supportive child-centred environment that enhances children's learning and development. This chapter has focused upon identifying the benefits of a mindful learning environment and how this can be achieved. Supporting self-regulation and creating an environment that enables adults to work with children to manage their emotions and learn to self-regulate, alongside their learning and development. An effective audit tool for practitioners was introduced to assess the current environment and its suitability in enhancing the emotional wellbeing of children. Additionally, by auditing the existing environment will enable practitioners to work more collaboratively to provide a warm and welcoming environment where everyone is valued and feels safe to explore their feelings and be accepted by knowledgeable and caring adults.

A four-step process was explained to begin creating a purposeful environment that aligns to and support children's emotions, needs and feelings. This chapter has identified that a mindful environment is one that promotes emotional wellbeing and provides stability for children according to their individual needs. This type of environment will provide children with adults who will provide emotional support and understanding of their feelings. Creating a mindful culture will enable a sense of children feeling safe and secure, enabling them to learn and develop with the confidence to explore and overcome challenges they may face.

Planning for the emotional environment should be part of the general cycle of planning, observing the children, noting their interests, needs and abilities and planning accordingly. This will help to ensure that the children within the provision have a sound and secure foundation to their emotional development, physical and mental health

References

Brookfield, S. (1995) *Becoming a Critically Reflective Teacher.* Josey-Bass: San Francisco.

Bruce, T. (2011) *EYFS Best Practice: All About Friedrich Froebel.* Accessed on 12 May 2021 at https://www.nurseryworld.co.uk/features/article/eyfs-best-practice-all-about-friedrich-froebel

DCSF (2008) *The National Strategies. Early Years Quality Improvement Support Programme.* Accessed on 19 March 2021 at https://foundationyears.org.uk/pedagogy-early-learning/quality-improvement/

Department for Education (DfE) (2009) *Every Child Matters.* Accessed on 12 February 2021 at https://assets.publishing.service.gov.uk/government/uploads/system/uploads/attachment_data/file/272064/5860.pdf

Department for Education (DfE) (2017) *Statutory Framework for the Early Years Foundation Stage.* Accessed on 12 January 2021 at https://www.icmec.org/wp-content/uploads/2018/01/EYFS_STATUTORY_FRAMEWORK_2017.pdf

Department for Education (DfE) (2020) *Development Matters: Non-statutory Curriculum Guidance for the Early Years Foundation Stage.* Accessed on 17 March 2021 at https://assets.publishing. service.gov.uk/government/uploads/system/uploads/attachment_data/file/1007446/ 6.7534_DfE_Development_Matters_Report_and_illustrations_web__2_.pdf

Early Years Alliance (2019) *Enabling Environment.* Accessed on 23 June 2021 at https://www. eyalliance.org.uk/enabling-environments

Early Years Matters (2017) Accessed on 12 May 2021 at https://www.earlyyearsmatters.co.uk/ our-services/school-and-nursery-improvement-partner/enabling-environments/emotional- /

Foundation Years (2012) *Getting Ready for the Revised EYFS – The Learning Environment.* Accessed on 16 July 2021 at https://foundationyears.co.uk/wp-content/uploads/2019/09/ Getting-Ready-for-the-Revised-EYFS.pdf

Laevers, F. (2005) *The Curriculum as Means to Raise the Quality of Early Childhood Education. Implications for Policy.* Accessed on 19 June 2021 at https://www.researchgate.net/publication/ 249047541_The_curriculum_as_means_to_raise_the_quality_of_early_childhood_ education_Implications_for_policy

Montessori Group Website (2022-2023). Accessed on 16 April 2022 at https://montessori-globaleducation.org/our-history/what-is-montessori/

Mukadam, Y. and Sutherland, H. (2018) *Supporting Toddlers' Wellbeing in Early Years Settings.* London: Jessica Kingsley Publishers.

Northamptonshire County Council, Early Years Improvement Team Learning Environment Audit: A tool for settings (2017) pdf. https://docslib.org/early-years-literacy-learning-environment-audit

Oxfordshire County Council (2008) *My Space Creating Enabling Environments for Young Children.* Accessed on 4 July 2022 at https://www2.oxfordshire.gov.uk/cms/sites/default/ files/folders/documents/childreneducationandfamilies/informationforchildcareproviders/ Toolkit/My_Space_Creating_enabling_environments_for_young_children.pdf

Sammons, P., Sylva, K., Melhuish, E., Siraj-Blatchford, I., Taggart, B., Barreau, S. and Grabbe, Y. (2007) *Effective Pre-school and Primary Education 3-11 Project (EPPE 3-11): Influences on Children's Development and Progress in Key Stage 2: Social/ Behavioural Outcomes in Year 5.* Research Report No. DCSF-RR007. Nottingham: DCSF Publications.

Shanker, S. (2020) Self-Regulation: The Early Years. Accessed on 23 November 2021 at https://self-reg.ca/wp-content/uploads/2021/05/infosheet_The-Early-Years.pdf

Siraj-Blatchford, I. (2002) *Cited in Department for Education (DfE) OECD (2015). Pedagogy in early childhood education and care (ECEC): An International Comparative Study of Approaches and Policies.*

Strong-Wilson, T. and Ellis, J. (2007) '*Children and Place: Reggio Emilia's Environment As Third Teacher*', *Theory into Practice*, 46(1), pp. 40–47. https://doi.org/10.1080/0040584070933654. Accessed on 20 November 2021 at https://tandfonline.com/

The MEHRIT Centre (2017) *Self-Reg School Toolkit.* Accessed on 13 October 2021 at https:// self-reg.ca/wp-content/uploads/2020/06/2017_18_FULL_TOOLKIT_TM.pdf

4 Mindfulness for staff wellbeing

Mindfulness is the awareness that arises from paying attention, on purpose, in the present moment and non-judgementally.

(Kabat–Zinn, 1994)

Aims of Chapter 4

This chapter aims to:

- Provide three mindfulness toolkits for staff in the early years.
- Identify what mental health and staff wellbeing are.
- Explore some of the current issues impacting staff wellbeing.
- Provide strategies to support staff's mental health and wellbeing.

Introduction

This chapter sets out to explore the role of mindfulness in supporting staff wellbeing with a set of practical and effective mindfulness activities that can be easily incorporated into the daily routine and work environment. The first toolkit provides activities that introduce staff to mindfulness in their day, followed by a second toolkit of activities for individuals to enhance their awareness of mindfulness and to practice daily activities that support a mindful approach to work. The third toolkit provides a set of mindfulness activities to support team building.

The benefits of mindfulness for adults are explained, with a more detailed introduction and evaluation of mindfulness in Chapter 1. The chapter goes on to

DOI: 10.4324/9780429030734-5

review how mindfulness as an intervention can support the emotional wellness of staff working in the early years by identifying some of the current issues and challenges affecting staff wellbeing. Finally, a range of strategies will be identified that can support settings to create better opportunities for mindful working.

Understanding the link between mindfulness and mental health

Many of us do not talk about our mental health, or we tend not to use those words to describe our emotional state. Identifying healthy coping strategies, such as mindfulness activities, can help us find the understanding and language to manage our mental health and wellbeing. Awareness is raised through initiatives such as Mental Health Awareness Month and Wellbeing initiatives created by employers to support their staff as the impact of the ongoing pandemic and fast-paced digital lifestyle that we are living in. 'Paying more attention to the present moment, to your own thoughts and feelings, and to the world around you – can improve your mental wellbeing' (NHS, 2022). This chapter sheds light and helps settings and staff focus on the mental health challenges and make sense of ways to improve mental health and staff wellbeing for a happier and healthier workforce.

Recap of what mindfulness is

Mindfulness is a quality that every human being already possesses, it's not something you have to conjure up, you just have to learn how to access it. Mindfulness is the basic human ability to be fully present, aware of where we are and what we're doing, and not overly reactive or overwhelmed by what's going on around us.

(Mindful, 2020)

Mindfulness is simply awareness of being in the present moment and experiencing life as it unfolds, one moment at a time. For example, when sitting down to drink your morning tea or coffee and really noticing how you are feeling in that moment, how your body is positioned in the chair, and how your tea or coffee tastes one sip at a time. This is the awareness called 'mindfulness'.

Professor Mark Williams, from the Oxford Mindfulness Centre, informs us that mindfulness means knowing what is going on inside and outside ourselves, moment by moment (NHS, 2022). At a personal level, the mindfulness activities in this chapter will guide you in becoming resourceful and resilient as an early years professional for your own wellbeing, to self-regulate your emotions and to work with more focus

Figure 4.1 **Woman in meditation.**

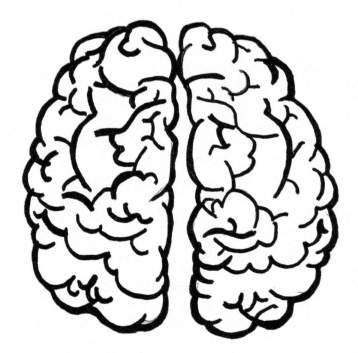

Figure 4.2 **Brain image in black and white.**

and clarity. At a professional level, you will benefit from a more mindful approach to work, especially when developing positive relationships with colleagues, children, families and other professionals.

A mindful approach to staff health and wellbeing

Staff health and wellbeing are critical to the success of any early years setting. Work can become an increasingly busy environment with no time to pause, reflect or rest physically and mentally. Learning mindfulness will help staff access quick tools to pause, reset and notice how they feel in the moment, adjusting and stepping back from the busyness of the daily routine for a few moments. Research provides strong evidence that practicing mindfulness changes the brain.

A longitudinal mindfulness study conducted by Hölzel et al. identified changes to regions of the brain and improvements to participants' mindfulness and wellbeing, as well as reducing their levels of perceived stress. This important study measured neurological changes during an eight-week mindfulness programme for participants. The eight-week programme was first created by Jon Kabat Zinn in the 1990s as an intervention consisting of weekly sessions including formal and guided mindfulness training exercises aimed at developing the capacity for mindfulness, including a body scan, yoga and a sitting meditation (Hölzel et al., 2011). Kabat-Zinn reminds us that by focussing on the breath, the idea is to cultivate attention on the body and mind as they are from moment to moment, to help with both physical and emotional pain (Booth, 2017).

Mindfulness for mental health

According to the World Health Organisation (WHO, 2022):

> Mental health is a state of wellbeing in which an individual realises his or her own abilities, can cope with the normal stresses of life, can work productively, and is able to make a contribution to his or her community.

Being mentally healthy is about how we think, feel and behave. Good mental health is particularly important in this digital fast-paced work, home and social environment that we find ourselves living in today. The term *mental health* is a positive concept that relates to the social and emotional wellbeing of an individual (Everymind, 2022). It is important to remember that *having good mental health is a state of overall wellbeing rather than just the absence of any mental illness.*

The Chartered Institute of Professional Development (CIPD) identifies the importance of caring for people's mental health in the workplace. They are one of many organisations that have signed up to the Mental Health at Work Commitment, created by the charity Mental Health at Work. For more information, see the link in the references (Mental Health at Work, 2019).

This initiative invites organisations to sign up to the 'mental health at work commitment', which provides a framework of six standards designed to help employers publicly declare that mental health is a priority for their organisation.

Early years settings can identify a mental health strategy for their staff by applying the six standards of the framework within their daily practice and aiming towards promoting employee wellbeing.

Recognising the importance of staff wellbeing

Staff wellbeing is about the holistic health of individuals and includes both their physical and emotional health. Promoting and supporting employee wellbeing needs to be at the heart of the workplace culture in the early years. The CIPD affirms that healthy workplaces help people flourish and reach their potential (CIPD, 2022).

Felton (2015) highlights that the Oxford English Dictionary states that wellbeing is 'the state of being comfortable, healthy, or happy', and recognises that although wellbeing relates to happiness, it also includes how satisfied people are with their lives and how in control they feel.

Reflective task: Consider your own wellbeing in the workplace and identify ways that staff wellbeing is currently supported in your setting:

....

....

....

With the average British worker spending about 34.5 hours per week in the workplace, almost one third of the week, it is evident that work can impact overall wellbeing (Perkbox, 2021).

Five Simple mindfulness activities to get started

This is the start of your daily mindfulness practice. These simple mindfulness activities will get you started on developing a more mindful state and directing your attention to the present moment.

You can do these either in your setting, as part of your daily routine, or during your break. Alternatively, build them into a staff meeting or training day.

Figure 4.3 **Hand holding brain.**

Activity one: Observe your thoughts for two minutes each day. Sit quietly for a few moments to notice what you are thinking. Just notice the range of thoughts currently in your mind, becoming aware of them without being drawn into them. If you have a worrying thought, you can visualise the thought drifting away on a cloud.

Activity two: Start to notice sounds around you in the external environment, then focus on and observe the facial expressions, colours, conversations and activities of children and other staff. Observe and listen with curiosity and without judgment.

Activity three: Notice your physical body and how you are feeling at this very moment. If you are sitting, how do you feel sitting on the chair? If you are walking, do you notice the breeze and the ground beneath you?

Activity four: Pay closer attention to your food and how it makes you feel. Learn to distinguish between emotional and physical hunger. Start by eating more slowly and without distractions, if you can. Eat with more awareness and engage your senses by noticing the colours, tastes, textures and smells of your food.

Activity five: Try something new this week, such as taking a slightly different or new route to work. Listen to songs and a podcast to stimulate your mind; cook a new meal or snack, changing up your daily habits. This helps you notice the world in a different way.

Figure 4.4 **Face of young girl.**

Current issues impacting staff wellbeing

This section identifies some of the current issues and challenges affecting staff well-being within the early years sector. As you may be aware, the daily role of an early year teacher (EYT) or early years practitioner (EYP) can be a continuous 'to do' list, ranging from implementing a broad and balanced curriculum, planning activities, observing children, monitoring and ensuring health and safety, auditing and planning, collaborative working, assessment and much, much more.

Issue one: Daily roles and responsibilities

Daily work pressures have continued to rise as the demands of providing high-quality care and education remain the priority points within the early years sector. Continuous changes to the landscape in early years policy and legislation have created ongoing challenges for staff to remain up-to-date, particularly since the start of the pandemic.

Alongside this, Ofsted inspections, low pay, long working hours and excessive paperwork and workloads traditionally contribute to the daily physical and mental health pressures recognised by the sector. These are all common aspects of working in the early years and will remain so, according to the Early Years Alliance Chief Executive, Neil Leitch (Oxtoby, 2021).

As many staff teams are aware, the Covid-19 pandemic has only exacerbated these issues, further affecting staff wellbeing. Good physical and mental health is now more vital than ever for individual staff. Leitch states that, 'We want the early years workforce to be in the best possible mental and physical health not just for themselves, but also for the benefit of the children in their care, as we know that young children pick up on the stresses and strains on the adults in their lives, which can in turn affect their wellbeing too'.

Reflective tasks:

a. Firstly, follow this link to the 'Foundation Years' website and explore the range of wellbeing and mental health resources available for early years settings: https://foundationyears.org.uk/2020/12/putting-wellbeing-at-the-heart-of-our-early-years-practice/

b. Next, identify and list at least three practical strategies that can be implemented to inform practice at your setting and improve understanding and commitment to staff wellbeing.

  1. ....

  2. ....

  3. ....

Many early years staff join the sector to make a difference in the lives of children, and unfortunately, the benefits and positives can sometimes be overshadowed by the increased responsibilities of individuals, affecting either or both the physical and mental health of individuals. The busy and fast-paced work environment demonstrates the ongoing 'demanding nature of caring for children combined with high workloads and poor pay' (Rawstrone, 2020).

It is therefore important to highlight here that one of the key responsibilities of a manager/owner of a setting is to balance the need to build a successful early years business with the need to support the emotional wellbeing of children and staff.

For many, staff wellbeing is now a key area for support and is viewed as integral to their success in the setting. The section towards the end of this chapter called 'Strategies for Supporting Staff Wellbeing' provides a framework that can be implemented to ensure that mental health and staff wellbeing are prioritised in your setting.

The Early Years Alliance relates to the importance of staff wellbeing, saying that 'We want the early years workforce to be in the best possible mental and physical health not just for themselves, but also for the benefit of the children in their care, as we know that young children pick up on the stresses and strains on the adults in their lives, which can in turn affect their wellbeing too' (Oxtoby, 2021).

It is important to summarise that interventions such as supervision, meetings, mindfulness practices and professional development opportunities need to be part of the wellbeing approach rather than seen as a cost to the business.

Issue two: Pandemic, health and closures

The pandemic resulted in the first lockdown in the United Kingdom since March 2020, with many nursery closures, staff furloughs and job losses. The changes and uncertainty within early years settings have been ongoing, with evident impact on staff wellbeing, particularly mental health. A survey by the EY Alliance identified that nursery staff reported how the pandemic had taken its toll on their mental health, with 50% stating that they felt unwell because of work-related stress during the pandemic year and 66% saying that the pandemic had impacted their wellbeing and mental health.

The role of the key person has continued to expand, and Heale (2021) identifies the complexities of this role when caring for a number of children of the same age who have a range of emotional needs. She states that the work can be highly demanding and complex, evoking feelings ranging from anxiety, uncertainty, frustration and exhaustion to pleasure, satisfaction and joy.

The pandemic in March 2020 identified new ways of working with settings, implementing new work processes and measures to support the health and wellbeing of children, staff and families. A range of challenges led by government interventions and pandemic repercussions, including closures, furloughs, redundancies and job losses. Much of this impacted staff, with research findings from the Anna Freud Centre survey (2021) reporting that the pandemic affected staff mental health and wellbeing. Findings showed that 50% of staff reported that they felt unwell as a result of work-related stress during the pandemic, and 66% reported that the pandemic had impacted their wellbeing and mental health. **Other issues affecting staff were:**

- Many felt unable to implement safety measures such as social distancing.

- Limited availability of personal protective equipment.

- Not being given home testing kits when these were introduced by the government.

- Not being prioritised for vaccination.

Letitia McCalla, the Professional Officer at Education Union Voice added that the above areas left many staff feeling anxious and less safe at work.

Although over a third (38%) of early years staff were placed on furlough between the months of November 2020 and February 2021 (Goddard, 2021), others continued to work to care for children of key workers or vulnerable families.

Many staff identified how the pandemic affected them with changes to the economy, job roles, inequality and poverty. Alongside this, educational attainment due to schools shutting down and home-schooling further impacts families and outcomes for children.

The Office for National Statistics also found that more women than men reported that homeschooling was having a negative impact on their well-being (53% compared with 45%). 'Settings have had to give staff time off to care for their own children and this has had an impact on them financially' (Walker, 2021).

The data from the survey discussed in this section was collated between 12 January 2021 and 2 February 2021, with findings from the responses of 1,458 nursery staff working in settings across England. The full survey findings are available and published by the Anna Freud Centre. To end on a more positive note, findings also indicated that nursery staff love their work and many believe their settings are actively engaging with staff mental health and achieving positive results.

Issue three: Recruitment and retention

Recruitment and retention of good-quality staff remain areas of concern for the sector. A survey conducted by the Early Years Alliance from October to November 2021 analysed the impact of staff recruitment and retention in the early years sector. Some of the key responses from the survey highlighted that the sector is reaching a crisis point with turnover rates between 11% and 15%, with more than eight in ten settings finding it difficult to recruit staff. This has resulted in around half of the settings limiting the number of children in early 2021. The survey also found that 96% of the early years workforce is female, with 14% living in relative poverty and 45% claiming state benefits or tax credits. The most worrying response in the survey was that over a third of respondents are actively considering leaving the sector. The results also identified that 'mental health and wellbeing in the sector also remains a significant concern, particularly in light of the ongoing Covid-19 pandemic' (Early Years Alliance, 2021).

To summarise, it is paramount for childcare settings to acknowledge and recognise these and other ongoing and new challenges in the workplace. There needs to be a commitment by management to provide the most effective and timely professional and practical support, including interventions such as mindfulness, supervision and training that are accessible for all staff's needs. To make this successful, staff engagement in mindfulness interventions and initiatives is crucial to developing a whole-setting approach to wellbeing.

This chapter will now provide three mindfulness toolkits to use in your early years setting and to support your own personal mindfulness practice.

- **Toolkit 1** is made up of five mindfulness activities to introduce into your early years setting.

- **Toolkit 2** is made up of ten daily mindfulness activities for early years staff.

- **Toolkit 3** is made up of ten team-building mindfulness activities for staff.

These mindfulness activities provide the opportunity for staff to practice daily mindfulness techniques for themselves and build their understanding and confidence when planning and implementing activities with children to develop healthy and positive relationships in the workplace.

MINDFULNESS TOOLKITS ONE

These mindfulness activities are a good introduction for EYPs and EYTs working in early years settings. **This first toolkit provides five introductory activities** that can be embedded into the daily routine for staff and children to bring more present moment awareness throughout your day.

1. **Reflect and check-in:** Start the day with a simple daily practice that gives you an opportunity to reflect on your emotions and your plans for the day ahead. The benefit of this activity is that it can be completed at any time, individually or in a group.

> 1. How am I feeling right now? (Begin the day with these reflective questions)
>
> 2. What am I grateful for in this moment? *(Make a list)*
>
> 3. What is my goal for today? *(Write this down)*
>
> 4. What do I need to achieve this?
>
> 5. How am I taking care of myself?
>
> 6. Five good qualities that I have are ....

2. **Thought cloud:** Each day, draw a cloud like the one here. Take a few minutes to bring yourself to the present moment. Notice your emotions right now and how they may be shaping your experience. Then fill your cloud with words or pictures that represent your feelings in this moment. A thought cloud enables you to let go of any worrying thoughts and feelings that you may have and release them from your mind.

Reflect on your thoughts and feelings for the week to see if they have changed or remained the same.

These questions can help you manage your thoughts and feelings and work on a more positive mindset:

1. Are there any thoughts that are making me feel upset/worried/anxious/sad?

2. How can I manage these thoughts? *(Tip: replace the anxious or worry thought with a positive one; for example, replace* 'I am worried about getting all my work completed this week' *to* 'I will plan my time to complete my work to the best of my ability, one task at a time'.

3. **Mindful walk:** Plan a regular walk at least three times per week. The simple intention is to become more aware of the environment around you by expanding your attention to sounds and tuning into your thoughts, feelings and any sensations in your body. If your mind wanders, allow yourself to connect to what is happening in the here and now.

Figure 4.5   **Woman with red jacket walking.**

4. **Gratitude list:** Make a list of five things that you are grateful for today. You can do this at any time. This mindful activity enables you to appreciate what you have by focusing on the positives, which in turn improves your mood. *Your list could include a walk, the sun shining, a friendship, the food you eat, health, family, etc.*

I am grateful for …

1.

2.

3.

4.

5. **Five-finger breathing:** This is a simple breathing exercise to help you start to notice your breath as it flows in and out of your body. Simply stand or sit where you are and follow your breath using your hand. Starting at the base of the thumb, breathe in (inhale) and breathe out (exhale) as you move down the thumb, continuing along each finger until you reach the other side of the hand.

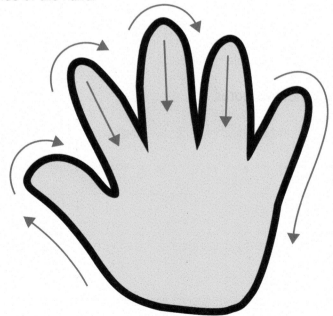

Figure 4.6 **Five-finger breathing.**

Toolkit one reflective notes

Activities that I found particularly effective and why:

....

....

....

Activities that I can introduce or adapt for children and staff in my setting:

....

....

....

MINDFULNESS TOOLKIT TWO: Ten individual mindfulness activites for Early Years Staff

Practising mindfulness daily can support staff become more aware of and manage their thoughts, feelings and emotions in the workplace. These activities can be weaved into the daily routine by individual staff or small groups of early years staff to reduce stress and bring clarity, calm and focus to your day.

Table 4.1 provides a toolkit of ten mindfulness activities for early years staff to implement into their daily routine.

Toolkit two reflective notes

Activities that I found particularly effective and why:

....

....

....

Activities that I can introduce or adapt for staff in my setting:

....

....

....

Table 4.1   Ten Mindfulness Activities for Early Years Staff

1   Mindful breathing exercise:

Start the day by noticing how you feel. Sitting or standing, acknowledge your thoughts and how your body feels in the moment.

- Next, bring your attention to your breath and take a long and gentle inhale through the nose.
- Lengthen your spine, allowing your breath to float into your belly and filling it up like a balloon.
- Now gently exhale through your mouth as if blowing out a candle, allowing the body to soften and relax. Repeat several times.

This breathing technique allows your body to tune into its rest and digest state (parasympathetic nervous system) and can be incorporated in your day at any time.

2   Morning yoga stretches:

Do you tend to start your day by going through mental checklists, scrolling through emails and checking social media?

Rethink your morning habit with some yoga stretches to bring flexibility and focus to the body and mind and ensure a more calming start to the day. Here are some yoga stretches to bring an uplift of energy and mindful movement to the start of your day.

- Bridge pose.
- Child's pose.

Figure 4.7   Woman seated in yoga rotation.

(Continued)

Table 4.1 Ten Mindfulness Activities for Early Years Staff (Continued)

***Figure 4.8* Woman in upward dog pose.**

- Cat and cow pose.

- Downward dog.

- Seated rotation.

- Upward dog pose.

Use this link to the Yoga Journal website for some uplifting yoga sequences: https://www.yogajournal.com/practice/uplifting-morning-yoga-flows/

3 Intention setting:

Intention setting is a useful activity to do at the start of the day. Set your alarm a few minutes earlier to allow time to sit with your thoughts and identify some intentions for the day ahead.

Writing down your intentions can be a good way to create a clear focus and help bring purpose to your day, aligning with your values and beliefs.

Start by asking yourself what you would like from the day ahead.

Here are some prompts for intention setting if this is new to you.

- I intend to listen to others before I speak.

(Continued)

Table 4.1   Ten Mindfulness Activities for Early Years Staff (Continued)

- I intend to enjoy being in the moment.
- I intend to find gratitude in this day.
- I intend to not take things personally.
- I intend to be kind and considerate.
- I intend to look after my mental health and wellbeing.
- I intend to enjoy the journey to work.
- I intend to take a few minutes outside and be in nature.
- I intend to practice mindful eating today.

Setting intentions is a great way to check in with yourself on a regular basis and awaken your body and mind from a sleep state. Cultivating this habit each morning can help you identify what is important as you go about your workday.

4   A mindful walk in nature:

Spend time in nature taking a mindful walk to help reduce any stress, worries, anxiety or overwhelm. A walk in nature, along the beach or any green outdoor space is a good way to relax.

- Walk slowly and notice what is going on around you.
- Really focus on each step you take.
- Think about how you are holding your body and moving your arms
- Notice the ground underneath your feet.
- Listen to the sounds around you: birds singing, the wind rustling through the leaves, etc.
- Feel the warmth of the sun or the coolness of the breeze.

Studies show that being outdoors or 'bringing nature into your everyday life can benefit both your mental and physical wellbeing' (https://www.mind.org.uk) including improved attention, lower stress and better mood.

5   A spot of mandala colouring:

Colouring is a creative way to practice mindfulness. Choose a simple picture or mandala design and take time for yourself to relax and enjoy the experience. It can be helpful if you find it hard to switch off from a busy day at work, as it allows the mind to slow down and become absorbed without strain or worry. Try it for yourself with this mandala pattern, taking time to select the colours and complete the pattern.

(Continued)

Table 4.1   **Ten Mindfulness Activities for Early Years Staff** *(Continued)*

Figure 4.9   **Mandala colouring in.**

Daily colouring allows the mind and body to relax as you become absorbed in choosing colours and work through completing your design. Looking at the intricacies in the pattern or picture keeps you in the moment.

6   **Body scan meditation:**

■ Set aside a time and place in your day where you can sit or lie comfortably without being distracted.

■ Find a peaceful place and make yourself comfortable, either sitting on a chair, lying on the floor or leaning against a wall to support your spine. From here, observe the movement of your breath and any physical sensations in your body.

(Continued)

Table 4.1   Ten Mindfulness Activities for Early Years Staff (Continued)

Figure 4.10   Cartoon of woman in yellow in seated yoga pose

- ■ Close your eyes and bring your attention to your toes, noticing any sensations.

- ■ Work up from your toes, bringing your awareness to each body part in turn: your feet, ankles, calves, knees, thighs, hips, chest, back, etc., all the way up to your head.

- ■ If your mind wanders, simply return to your breath, notice what you were thinking and then return your focus back to scanning the body.

A regular body scan helps to reduce stress, decrease muscle tension and encourage self-awareness of sensations and feelings that we may ignore or not notice. It encourages you to enter a state of 'being in the present moment'.

7   Mindful eating:

Are you eating mindfully? Eating your food mindfully is not a new concept. Mindful eating is about taking time to sit and eat without distractions so that you can immerse yourself in the practice of eating your food slowly, enjoying the tastes, smells and flavours of your food. Taking time to eat without rushing or multi-tasking improves digestive function, reduces overeating and provides a more enriching experience.

(Continued)

Table 4.1   Ten Mindfulness Activities for Early Years Staff (Continued)

Mindful eating process:

■ Sit down, even if it is only for ten minutes.

■ Turn off any devices and give food your full attention.

■ Observe and notice each bite.

■ Enjoy the taste, smell and texture.

■ Chew your food rather than rushing.

■ Follow this daily to make it a positive lifestyle habit.

Eating mindfully makes us more present and aware of the food that we are eating. It also enables us to become aware of hunger cues and recognise if we are eating because we are physically hungry or emotionally hungry.

8 **The power of observational drawing:**

An observational drawing is a perfect way to reconnect with the joy of being creative and artistic. Choose an object such as a bright and colourful flower.

■ Take time to observe and scrutinise the flower, looking at the detail within the petals, stem and leaves.

■ How delicate is the flower?

■ What shape are the petals?

■ How does it smell?

■ Have a go at drawing the flower, taking your time to start at the centre using soft and gentle strokes.

■ Take your time and absorb yourself in the activity.

Drawing supports creativity and enhances focus and concentration. It is also a process that taps into your creative brain and boosts your mood.

9 **Daily journaling:**

Journaling is a mindful way to make plans, reflect and write to clear the mind and get everything down on paper. It is a reflective process that enables you to write down your thoughts, goals, plans and achievements.

■ The act of 'writing down' how you are feeling and your daily intentions is both cathartic and enables us to commit to what is important in life. This works well if you find enjoyment in the writing process.

■ First thing in the morning or before bedtime are good times to journal; however, choose a time that works for you.

■ Buy yourself a journal, notepad or book that becomes an important part of your daily routine for mindful working and being.

(Continued)

Table 4.1 **Ten Mindfulness Activities for Early Years Staff (*Continued*)**

Daily journaling provides a perfect time to sit and reflect and make notes that you can read and help you be a better version of yourself, bringing intention and clarity to each day.

10 Yoga – Sun salutation:

Today, many of us spend a larger part of our day indoors or sitting at a desk. A sedentary lifestyle can present a range of health problems in life. Yoga is a form of exercise that you can choose to do at home, at work or by attending a class.

Yoga means to unite the body and mind. The sun salutation is a flow of postures that can be done for as little as 2 minutes or for as long as 30 minutes, any time of the day. If time is an issue or you are new to yoga, you can start with one round of sun salutations to warm the muscles and improve blood flow while stretching and preparing your body and mind for the day ahead.

Figure 4.11 **Woman standing in warrior pose.**

The sun salutation sequence is usually made up of 12 postures that support your balance, flexibility and body strength and help you focus on deep breathing as you set your intention for the day. Elizarde (2021) provides a video and article on the Yoga Journal website. Refer to the link in the reference list at the end of this chapter to access a 'Sun Salutation' practice that you can follow if you are a beginner or experienced in yoga and mindfulness. *Yoga and stretching can help improve blood flow, increase calmness in the mind and energise your body for the day ahead. Regular aerobic exercise can reduce anxiety by making your brain's fight or flight system less reactive, thereby reducing stress and leading to a greater sense of wellbeing.*

Mindfulness staff survey (audit)

Questionnaires and surveys are one of the simplest ways to understand the needs of staff. From the results, tailored support can be provided to support individuals and groups towards better mental health. It is, however, important to regularly survey staff to establish current needs. Here is a sample survey that you can use or adapt to audit the mental health and wellbeing of staff in the setting.

Table 4.2 provides a sample survey for auditing staff mental health and wellbeing at supervision meetings or alongside other wellbeing initiatives for staff.

A regular wellbeing survey is a simple and effective way to promote a whole-system approach to good mental health and wellbeing. It enables managers and senior staff to reach out to staff and gather data that can be analysed and used to provide continuous professional development (CPD) opportunities and support in reducing work stress and poor mental health. According to a report by The Health and Safety Executive (2021), education professionals and teaching staff had one

Table 4.2   **Sample Survey for Auditing Staff Mental Health and Wellbeing**

Question	Comment
1. How are you feeling today? physically and mentally	
2. What do you enjoy most about your job?	
3. Are there any areas that you need support or training with?	
4. Explain the support or training that would most benefit you?	
5. Are you eating and sleeping well?	
6. Do you feel equipped to manage your mental health and wellbeing at work?	
7. Would you be open to trying yoga and mindfulness activities at work?	
8. What is taking up most of your headspace (thinking) at work this week?	
9. How can we support you further in your role to improve your wellbeing?	
10. Do you take time to exercise and stretch?	

of the highest rates of work-related stress, depression and anxiety in Britain over the three-year period from 2018–2019 to 2020–2021. These professionals cited workload pressures such as tight deadlines, too much responsibility and a lack of managerial support as the main factors that caused them work-related stress, depression and anxiety (The Health and Safety Executive, 2021).

Five strategies for improving staff mental health and wellbeing

Following on from the audit, regular team meeting discussions and ongoing staff supervision and appraisals, managers can work with their teams to develop strategies that support the mental health and wellbeing of all staff in their early years setting.

These five strategies can be applied in early years practice to transform and support wellbeing policies and practices in your setting.

1. **Instil the intention of looking forward to the day ahead, one task at a time.**
   Empower staff to start the day by accepting what is coming up and to be fully present for each task, conversation and thing that they do instead of worrying about what's next or what has happened in the past. This habit of 'looking forward' to the day enables you to embrace the day instead of trying to fight the day.

   When we become anxious about the day ahead, we add unnecessary stress to our lives, and this can set a negative tone for the day. Instead of stressing, look forward to the day ahead and intentionally surrender to the tasks and responsibilities that you have to do in a positive way.

2. **Develop a staff wellbeing framework.**
   A good starting point for nursery owners, managers and senior management is to create a wellbeing framework for their setting to improve the overall mental and physical wellbeing of staff. **Here is a framework for early years settings to consider based on the plan-do-review model.**

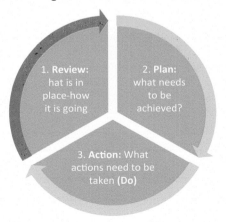

Figure 4.12 **Three-step staff wellbeing framework.**

1. **REVIEW: Consider what is currently in place within the setting:**

   - Do you have a setting policy to support staff wellbeing and mental health?

   - Identify current mental health and wellbeing issues impacting staff.

   - What is currently in place to support staff and how is this going?

   - Identify current measures in place to reduce workload and enable staff participation in wellbeing activities.

2. **PLAN: What actions need to be taken:**

   - Review the supervision process and staff meetings to include staff wellbeing as an agenda item.

   - Carry out an audit/survey to identify the issues and challenges. Use this assessment tool to review it on a quarterly basis.

   - Identify key priorities and include them in the improvement plan.

   - What is currently in place to support staff, and how is this going?

3. **ACTIONS: Plan what needs to be set up and achieved:**

   - Develop or create a policy for staff mental health and wellbeing.

   - Identify a lead person to disseminate information, deliver training and provide guidance for staff wellbeing.

   - How can the work environment promote a more open culture about mental health?

   - Develop mindfulness activities, resources and interventions to signpost staff to mindfulness in the workplace.

Actions and follow-up work relating to the Plan-do-review process:

---

4. **Recognise and support mental health at work.**
   Early years settings can identify a mental health strategy for their staff by applying the six standards of the CIPD. These standards are designed to help employers

publicly declare that mental health is a priority for them to promote wellbeing for all employees.

The six standards are as follows:

1. Prioritise mental health at work by developing a programme of activity.

2. Ensure that work design and organisational culture drive positive mental health outcomes.

3. Promote an open culture around mental health.

4. Increase organisational confidence and capability.

5. Provide mental health tools and support.

6. Internal and external reporting to increase transparency.

5. **Create a wellbeing plan for your early years setting (Table 4.3).**
   In applying the Wellbeing Plan above, underpinned by the six CIPD standards, here are some practical strategies that can be considered in terms of developing a culture that embodies staff wellbeing and provides effective and timely guidance, support and interventions for staff:

1. Daily opportunities for staff to talk openly and in confidence about their feelings, emotions and wellbeing. This could be related to work or a personal issue. This promotes a wellbeing culture and begins to remove the stigma attached to discussing mental health in the workplace.

Table 4.3 **Sample Wellbeing Plan for Early Years Settings**

This sample plan can be adapted for your setting

Priority 1:	Include mindfulness strategies in the setting mental health policy
Priority 2:	Staff supervision with a safe space to reflect on aspects of wellbeing
Priority 3:	Weekly yoga classes and training opportunities.
Priority 4:	Work wellbeing events for staff, e.g., brunches, pamper sessions and social events
Priority 5:	Workload and job role support, reviews, wellbeing surveys and open-door sessions with an allocated setting wellbeing/mental health lead

2. Enable staff to share their concerns in a safe and supportive environment, as this gives them the confidence to voice their ideas and raise issues confidently within their work environment. Consider a regular wellbeing agenda item at a staff meeting, team briefing, supervision or INSET days.

3. A 'Working Together' approach to understanding mindfulness as a means towards creating opportunities for staff to improve their wellbeing and mental health. *For example, daily mindful activities; whole-setting mindful moments such as a mindfulness bell; and an open-door policy encouraging staff to talk and share their feelings, emotions, ideas and issues.*

MINDFULNESS TOOLKET THREE: Ten team building mindfulness activities.

These activities can be introduced at team meetings or discussable activities at training sessions, supervision or team briefings. The activities enable and support early years settings to look holistically at the mental, physical and emotional health of the staff team to promote wellbeing and enhance performance at work.

1. Write a gratitude letter

Who are you grateful for in your life?
Call to mind someone who has done something for you for which you are extremely grateful, and you would like to express your gratitude to them in a letter. Make a list of at least three people and choose to write to one of them. Describe specifically what they did and why you are grateful to this person. Also include how this has affected you as a person. Speak from the heart. If it is another staff member, then you can give the letter to them; otherwise, you can send or give the person the letter.
Benefits: This is a powerful mindfulness activity and process that can enable us to share our gratitude in a meaningful way.

2. One-minute mindful re-set

A busy mind can leave us feeling mentally tired and lacking energy. Inviting mindful pauses into the daily routine enables the opportunity to reset and focus on how we are feeling mentally and physically.

Take the next minute to sit or stand in a comfortable position. Take three long deep breaths, inhaling and exhaling to centre the body and mind.

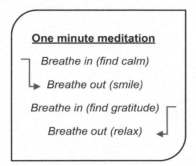

One minute meditation

Breathe in (find calm)

Breathe out (smile)

Breathe in (find gratitude)

Breathe out (relax)

Notice as you start to become more alert and present to what is happening around you. Become aware of the sounds and sights as your senses are heightened in present-moment awareness. Then next time you are working with children, sitting in a meeting or listening to a conversation you will be more connected and attentive to the situation and experiences as they unfold. This is a skill to practice with this simple mindfulness exercise.

Benefits: This activity brings awareness to the present moment and gives you a moment to check in with how you feel. At the same time, you will start to improve mental focus, concentration and clarity of mind.

3. Petal practice

This simple mindfulness practice can be done when you have one minute to reset and take a pause in your day.

Start by sitting on a chair or somewhere comfortable. Lengthen your spine and start to notice your breath. Make loose fists with both hands as you rest them on your lap. Imagine both of your hands opening and closing like the petals of a beautiful flower, inhaling as you close your hands and exhaling on the opening of your hands. Follow the breath and visualise your favourite flower closing gently on the inhale and blossoming beautifully on the exhale. You can hold a real flower if you prefer.

Benefits: This is a good way to focus on your breath and reduce any doubts, worries or feelings of anger or overwhelm. This practice also slows down your thinking and enables the brain to feel less cluttered, improving brain function.

Figure 4.13   Pink flower.

4. Group yoga session

These power yoga poses aim to build strength and flexibility in the body and create calm and focus in the mind. One staff can lead and guide staff to do the following stretches and poses. This activity can also be planned as part of the daily routine for children.

Lay out some mats or simply set up an area in the outdoor area to enjoy a few mindful minutes to balance and reset.

Balancing work life and home life and everything in between can seem hectic, so a ten-minute morning or afternoon yoga practice for yourself, the team or with children is a calming and relaxing way to take care of your mental and physical health on a daily basis. You can make laminated pictures for children to follow along with each of the poses to music indoors or outdoors.

Benefits: Yoga improves physical and mental health, including flexibility and strength, and brings calm and relaxation to the body through the movements and stillness.

Figure 4.14   **Grid showing 15 yoga postures.**

5. Tune into your listening!

This is a five-minute adapted practice from Collard (2014).

The aim of this activity is to slow down your thinking and become more aware of your mind. You can practice this to control and strengthen your mind.

■ The goal of any mindfulness practice is to experience life as it unfolds.

■ For this practice, it is important to stay present and calm and not slip back into thinking or worrying mode. Think of a point of focus that you can direct your mind to and anchor your awareness.

■ Take a seat, closing your eyes or gazing down at a focal point.

■ Allow sounds to enter your awareness, letting them pass by like clouds floating past in the sky. Become aware, but don't dwell on the sounds or thoughts; don't name them or relate them to any experience. When we get involved with sounds, this triggers our left (thinking) brain rather than our right (feeling) brain. Just be present for the sounds.

■ You may notice that your hearing becomes more focused; You may at times notice thoughts arising. This is the nature of the mind as it tends to get busy even when we don't want it to. So when you notice your mind wandering, gently and without judgment, return your awareness and your mindfulness to simply listening and observing your thoughts.

- Your breathing may get longer and deeper and the mind and body may become more relaxed; time and where you are right now may not seem to matter to you. If there is no change or 'nothing happens' for you and you feel that you are just sitting, then that is okay too.

- This practice will unfold differently each time you do it. There is no particular outcome; just see how it feels for you without judgment.

6. Five senses exercise

You can practice mindfulness everyday very quickly in nearly any situation. All that is needed is to notice something using your five senses. Give this a go!

- **Notice five things that you can *see*.**
  Look around you and bring your attention to five things that you can see. Choose things that you don't normally notice, like a shadow, a small object or a small crack in the pavement.

Figure 4.15 **Cartoon woman seated on a blue cushion – Hand on tummy and upper body.**

■ **Notice four things that you can _feel_.**
Bring awareness to four things that you are currently feeling, like the seat that you are sitting on, the feeling of the breeze on your skin or the smooth surface of a table you are resting your hands on.

■ **Notice three things you can _hear_.**
Take a moment to listen and note three things that you hear around you. This can be birds chirping, the sound of traffic nearby or distant music.

■ **Notice two things you can _smell_.**
Bring your awareness to smells that you usually filter out, whether they are pleasant or unpleasant. How do they make you feel, and what do they remind you of?

■ **Notice one thing you can _taste_.**
Focus on one thing that you can taste when you eat or take a sip of drink. How does it taste? Sweet, sour, hot or cold. Explore and notice with more awareness.

7. Single-tasking not multi-tasking

Single-tasking is the opposite of multi-tasking. It is about focussing on one task only, as much as you would like to be doing many tasks all at once! Single-tasking requires you to fully engage your mind with the task that you are working on.

For example, writing observations requires focus and concentration so that the task is completed to a good standard. To complete this daily task mindfully, you must focus on:

■ Your posture and how you are sitting or standing.

■ Notice how your body feels and how you are breathing.

■ Gather your thoughts about what you have observed, then start writing without feeling rushed.

■ Keep focussed on the task and do not get tempted to start another task.

Note how it feels when you have completed one task completely and then move on to the next with a more mindful approach.

8. What do you enjoy? Get creative

Doing something creative can really help you feel joyful and calm. This activity supports the creative process and improves mental health by:

- Distracting you from worrying thoughts.

- Support positive emotions.

- Stimulate your creativity and senses.

Find some time, even a few minutes, to do something creative. This will give you an outlet and a focus for your emotions. You can try activities such as drawing, painting, playing a musical instrument, sewing or baking. The most important thing to remember is to focus on enjoying the process of 'doing' and not worry about the finished product.

9. Identify your stress triggers

Understanding what makes you feel stressed and overwhelmed can really help you anticipate issues as they arise. You are then in a better position to reflect and consider ways to resolve or manage the issues or worries. Being prepared can make a difference.

Now take time to reflect on events, situations and feelings that contribute to your stress, such as a situation at work, a person, an upcoming event, a relationship or an ongoing problem or feeling.

Write down your three stress triggers here and then think of strategies to manage them. It may be as simple as a breathing technique or focussing the mind on a new hobby or task.

Table 4.4 provides an opportunity to identify stress triggers and reflect on a strategy to manage each stressor.

Table 4.4 Identified Stress Triggers with Strategies to Manage Each Stressor

Stress trigger:	Strategy to manage the stressor:
1.	
2.	
3.	

10. Time to reflect

As a group or staff team, it is important to reflect and write out a list of your daily tasks, achievements and goals for the week. Questions to consider can include:

Table 4.5 provides reflective questions that will enable staff to create smart and achievable goals, and tasks, as well as recognise and celebrate achievements.

Table 4.5   Table of Weekly Goals, Achievements and Tasks

- My daily tasks this week are:

- My achievements so far this week are:

- My **health** goal this week is:

- My **mind** goal this week is:

- My **work** goal this week is:

- Which important tasks do I need to complete this week:

- How manageable are these tasks, and who can support me:

- How can my manager support me with my work and responsibilities this week:

- Which mindfulness activities from this chapter can I do to improve my wellbeing this week:

Figure 4.16   Woman seated with seven icons around her.

To extend this activity further, think of aspects of the day or tasks that could be done differently to enable you to be better organised so that you are not rushing from one task to another.

Next, review these questions and discuss your thoughts and responses with the team:

■ What currently makes you feel stressed or anxious at work and why?

■ Do you feel supported in your job?

■ Do you feel valued when you are at work?

■ Who is responsible for your happiness at work?

Case study: Day Nursery Setting

Sue Chesson, identifies effective strategies for staff wellbeing. She suggests that 'If you want staff to be nurturing then you need to nurture them – show you appreciate them, make sure they're not overloaded and ensure that they know they can talk freely' (Heale, 2021).

Strategies for staff wellbeing:

1. Nurture staff and ensure they have opportunities to talk freely with you.

2. Taking a few minutes at the start of the day to find out how staff are feeling and catch up on news.

3. Supervision on a regular basis as a formal structure to support staff support.

Chesson adds that 'building in supervision time adds cost to a business in terms of time and physical space. But it is surely worthwhile if it helps reduce anxiety'.

These strategies are supported by Peter Elfer, Principal Lecturer at the University of Roehampton, who says,

There is very little space in nurseries – no time, no meeting place and, most of all, not always a supportive or conducive culture – for speaking about feelings. Nursery staff have this pivotal role and yet they're given no physical or mental space for reflection.

(Heale, 2021)

Despite the growing daily demands, the most important message in this brief case study is for staff to feel reassured that they can come forward to discuss mental health concerns and to know that those concerns will be taken seriously. With the growing knowledge and support offered in the sector, the approach to staff wellbeing will continue to grow.

Conclusion

Resourcing yourself with a strong mindfulness practice is the core purpose of this chapter. Key terms relating to staff wellbeing are defined and explored at the outset, including mental health, wellbeing, mindfulness and mediation. The value of introducing a mindfulness approach to support the mental health and wellbeing of early years staff is discussed. A range of practical mindfulness activities are set out for staff to access and practice to manage their mental health and wellbeing when dealing with personal or professional issues. The physical and psychological benefits of mindfulness are provided, along with strategies and a plan-do-review model for owners, managers and senior management to consider when developing wellbeing policies and improving the mental health outcomes of their staff.

Some of the current issues impacting staff wellbeing, including the pandemic and staff recruitment, are highlighted and explained with a set of team-building mindfulness activities and simple practices to develop a mindful approach to working in any early years setting to embed the process of 'being mindful' rather than 'doing mindfulness'.

References

Booth, R. (2017) *People are Losing Their Minds. That is What we Need to Wake Up To.* Accessed on 6 January 2022 at https://www.theguardian.com/lifeandstyle/2017/oct/22/mindfulness-jon-kabat-zinn-depression-trump-grenfell

Chartered Institute of Professional Development (CIPD) (2022) *Supporting the Mental Health at Work Commitment.* Accessed on 27 May 2022 at https://www.cipd.co.uk/knowledge/culture/well-being/mental-health-at-work-commitment#gref

Collard, P. (2014) *The Little Book of Mindfulness: 10 Minutes a Day to Less Stress, More Peace.* Octopus Publishing Group: London.

DfE (2003) Every Child Matters. Accessed on 23 April 2021 at https://assets.publishing.service.gov.uk/government/uploads/system/uploads/attachment_data/file/272064/5860.pdf

Early Years Alliance (2021) *Breaking Point Survey.* Accessed on 14 July 2022 at https://www.eyalliance.org.uk/sites/default/files/breaking_point_report_early_years_alliance_2_december_2021.pdf

Elizarde, T. (2021) *Yoga Journal. Love Sun Salutations? This is the Practice for you.* Accessed on 5 June 2021 at https://www.yogajournal.com/live-be-yoga-featured/sun-salutation/

Everymind (2022) *Understanding Mental Health.* Accessed on 18 May 2022 at https://everymind.org.au/understanding-mental-health

Felton, L. (2015) *What is Wellbeing, How Can We Measure it and How Can We Support People to Improve It.* Accessed on 17 June 2022 at https://www.mentalhealth.org.uk/explore-mental-health/blogs/what-wellbeing-how-can-we-measure-it-and-how-can-we-support-people-improve-it

Goddard, C. (2021) *Staff Healthy & Wellbeing: Part 1 - The State We're in.* Accessed on 26 May 2022 at https://www.nurseryworld.co.uk/features/article/staff-health-well-being-part-1-the-state-we-re-in

Heale, S. (2021) *Juggling Priorities: Why Great Early Years Settings Care about Staff Wellbeing.* Accessed on 14 June 2022 at https://www.teachearlyyears.com/images/uploads/article/managers-role.pdf

Kabat-Zinn, J (1994) *Wherever You Go. There You Are: Mindfulness Meditation in Everyday Life.* London: Piatkus.

Mental Health at Work (2019) *The Mental Health at Work Commitment.* Accessed on 24 October 2022 at https://www.mentalhealthatwork.org.uk/commitment/

Mental Health Foundation (2021) *What is Wellbeing, How Can We Measure it and How Can We Support People to Improve it.* Accessed on 7 February 2022 at https://www.mentalhealth.org.uk/explore-mental-health/blogs/what-well-being-how-can-we-measure-it-and-how-can-we-support-people-improve-it

Mindful (2020) *What is Mindfulness?* Accessed on 23 June 2021 at https://www.mindful.org/what-is-mindfulness/

National Health Service (NHS) (2022) *Mindfulness.* Accessed on 5 July 2022 at https://www.nhs.uk/mental-health/self-help/tips-and-support/mindfulness/

Oxtoby, K. (2021) *Time to Make Staff Wellbeing a Policy.* Accessed on 18 June 2022 at https://www.earlyyearseducator.co.uk/news/article/time-to-make-staff-wellbeing-a-policy

Perkbox (2021) *The What, Why and How of Workplace Wellbeing.* Accessed on 12 February 2021 at https://www.perkbox.com/uk/platform/perks/the-what-why-and-how-of-workplace-wellbeing

Rawstrone, A. (2020) *Staff Well-Being – Well Supported.* Accessed on 5 May 2022 at https://www.nurseryworld.co.uk/features/article/leadership-staff-well-being-well-supported

The Health and Safety Executive Report (published 16 December 2021) https://www.hse.gov.uk/statistics/csausdis/stress.pdf

Walker, A. (2021) *Closures of Nurseries Increase as Pressures of Pandemic Take Hold.* Accessed on 5 November 2022 at https://ndna.org.uk/news/closures-of-nurseries-increase-as-impact-of-pandemic-takes-hold/

World Health Organisation (WHO) (2022) *Mental Health.* Accessed on 7 January 2023 at https://www.who.int/news-room/fact-sheets/detail/mental-health-strengthening-our-response

5 Mindfulness activities for children in early years

Aims of Chapter 5

This chapter aims to:

■ Introduce the concept of mindfulness to children in the early years.
■ Provide a bank of mindfulness activities and techniques for children to access.
■ Enable early years professionals (EYPs) and early years teachers (EYTs) to plan a wellbeing early years curriculum that links to the early years foundation stage.
■ Consider age and stage appropriate mindfulness activities to help children self-regulate and improve their wellbeing and mental health.

Figure 5.1   **Boy sitting on grass with book.**

DOI: 10.4324/9780429030734-6

Introduction

There is an increasing awareness within educational settings about the impact of mindfulness on children's mental health. With around one in six children having experienced a mental health problem (NHS Digital, 2020), the practice of mindfulness has been incorporated into settings to support children's mental health and wellbeing. Wedge (2018) identifies seven key evidence-based ways that mindfulness can help children by:

1. Enabling the habit of focussing on the present moment and ignoring distractions.

2. Teaching children to stay calm in stressful times.

3. Promoting happiness by lowering social anxiety and stress.

4. Promoting patience.

5. Creating good habits for the future.

6. Improving executive functions in their brain such as cognitive control and memory.

7. Improving their attentiveness and impulse control.

This chapter will introduce you to a range of effective mindfulness activities and techniques that you can introduce into the daily practice for children and staff in your setting. The activities are designed to be implemented as and when required by EYPs and EYTs and can be incorporated in a purposeful way to create mindful opportunities for a child or group of children that focus on developing the skills to help children regulate their emotions, improve attention, focus and feel calm.

The chapter will draw on the relevance of mindfulness and how it can be built into daily planning and linked to the EYFS prime areas of learning and development. Many of the activities and techniques can engage children with special educational needs and can be adapted for babies and children, offering you practical ways to create mindful moments into the daily routine to meet individual needs and to suit the context and needs of all children.

Mindfulness for children

The actual practice of mindfulness is very simple, and the children of all ages benefit from mindfulness activities. EYPs and EYTs are able to support children by creating mindful opportunities to help children learn to recognise and regulate their emotions, feel calm and be present to their surroundings, feelings and physical wellbeing.

In recent years there has been an increase in our awareness, understanding and scientific research about the impact of mindfulness on our mental health (Currid, 2020). Brain scanning technologies have identified that the physical structure of the brain can change when a person practises mindfulness regularly (Hölzel et al., 2011).

Although there is very little research on how to effectively deliver mindfulness approaches within early years settings, there are studies reviewing the evidence of mindfulness-based interventions and identifying the impact on children and young people.

1. A literature review by Nieminen and Sajaniemi (2016) provides an overview of nine mindfulness intervention studies with 200 children as participants, aged 3–15 years of age. Some of the key findings from the review identify a range of outcomes, including improved sustained attention, better intellectual skills, improved working memory and concentration and physical health.

   This study points out that teaching mindfulness-based techniques to children and young people needs to be different to teaching adults, in that methods, materials and activities are generally more playful, with a focus on fun, and shorter times for sitting quietly.

2. A year-long study conducted by Holt et al. (2022) in the form of an action research project with one early year's setting explored how early years practitioners could effectively deliver mindfulness. The challenges, impact, implementation and findings show the importance of developing effective and inclusive mindfulness approaches, reflecting on practice and working collaboratively and creating a supportive community.

As we know, a positive emotional environment is one that promotes children's emotional wellbeing and supports their individual needs. The benefits of mindfulness within the emotional environment include:

- Creating spaces for children that provide opportunities to sit and be calm, without distractions.

- A toolkit of activities that engage children to connect with their body and mind, understanding and becoming aware of their emotions.

- Giving children techniques to use when they need to reduce anxiety, stress and manage their feelings in every-day situations or during a transition.

- Staff using a range of interventions such as music to introduce mindfulness, particularly for children with more limited language skills.

- Staff modelling techniques that children practise regularly so that they are more likely to be able to draw on these naturally when needed.

The role of the adult

By developing your own mindfulness knowledge and practice, as detailed in chapter four, will enable you to provide quality mindful experiences for children in your setting. By starting with yourself and sharing developing staff wellbeing, EYPs and EYTs will have a better understanding of how to practice mindfulness and notice the benefits for themselves, before introducing the concepts to children. From this knowledge and self-practice adults in the setting can build mindfulness into the daily routine for children with simple activities such as belly breathing, eating more mind-fully at mealtimes or encouraging children to engage with their surroundings in a more mindful way. It is important to remember that mindfulness is not always about planning a specific activity; it is about building mindful moments into the daily routine such as moving our bodies with more awareness, being still or listening to music and sounds. Consider the age and stage of development of the children and remember to keep instructions simple and use words that children will understand or visualisations and pictures that support and foster a positive atmosphere for mindfulness.

By introducing babies and young children to moments of calm and quiet times during their day alongside play enables their brain to make neural connections in an environment that is more emotionally positive. The goal of mindfulness is to

Figure 5.2   **Girl sitting on tree.**

give children the tools they need to connect with what is going on in their world in the present moment. It is also about empowering them to accept their thoughts and feelings and for healthy habits for coping with all the big emotions they may experience (Gill, 2020).

Ackerman's (2022) research confirms how mindfulness can:

- Mitigate the effects of bullying.

- Enhance focus in children with ADHD.

- Reduce attention problems.

- Improve mental health and wellbeing.

- Improve social skills when taught and practiced with children and adolescents.

Getting started with mindfulness: A wellbeing curriculum in practice

As a starting point, it is important to identify that early years settings are integral to raising the wellbeing of children alongside government guidance, and working with parents, families, communities and other professionals.

An effective way to support the wellbeing of children is to provide a wellbeing-based curriculum incorporating mindfulness activities that enhance children's mental health and emotional wellbeing, rather than focussing on outcomes. As children's brain and nervous system develops, they need positive experiences and a range of activities that support self-regulation skills. High-quality early years provision connects all areas of learning and development and supports children to become resilient and independent learners. The pandemic reduced opportunities for children's holistic development as they adjusted to the ongoing uncertainty and changes to their care, education and daily life. Post pandemic the focus has shifted from the immediate impacts towards children's recovery and their future. The mindfulness activities in this chapter are a positive approach step forward for EYPs and EYTs to understand the importance of developing a wellbeing focus and to support self-regulation as part of children's early learning.

Developing mindfulness activities into the early years curriculum for babies and children will provide many benefits including creating a more balanced approach to learning and provision of activities, experiences and tools that promote emotional wellbeing and positive mental health.

With continued impact of the pandemic, it is right that professionals working in early years look to the future and ensure that mental health is prioritised. A Department for Education (DfE, 2022a) report highlights the experiences of children and young

Figure 5.3 **Face of girl looking downwards.**

people aged five plus throughout the pandemic during the 2020–2021 academic year. This confirms that government focus for several years has been to support the well-being of children and young people. The impact of the coronavirus disease in 2020 (the Covid-19 pandemic) emphasised the importance of supporting our children and young people's wellbeing, which is why it remains a central part of the Department for Education's plans for recovery.

Long term the mindfulness activities will become a toolkit that can be used towards building resilience, compassion, calm and attention and all essential qualities enabling children to express their feelings now and into adulthood. The ideas and activities in this chapter have culminated from planned and impromptu activities that I have implemented within a range of early years settings and primary school environments for babies and children aged from 6 months to 5 years old.

Mindfulness to support children's feelings and emotions

Children experience a range of emotions on a day-to-day basis. The role of the EYTs and EYPs is to enable all children to express their feelings and emotions within a safe and supportive environment.

The benefits of self-regulation for children includes:

■ Inviting children to learn the skill in acknowledging emotions.

■ Working with adults who model and support children to manage their feelings.

■ Using coping strategies to regulate emotions and feelings.

■ Working within The EYFS requirements.

■ Enhancing wellbeing of children.

Five starter mindfulness activities for children

Here are five mindfulness activities to spark the joy of present moment awareness for children in your setting.

These are just a few ideas to get you started and give you confidence to support children on their mindfulness journey whilst improving their mental health and wellbeing. The activities are suitable mainly for children 20 months to 5 years of age.

Figure 5.4 **Sun black arrow and smiley face.**

1. Rainbow of emotions – Emotion Wheel

This is a simple starter activity for the day and provides a helpful way for children to recognise the feelings and emotions that they experience during the day. The Emotion Wheel can be used by EYPs and EYTs as a visual prompt to discuss and support children to identify and share their emotions rather than suppress them.

This activity idea is inspired by Robert Plutchik's Emotion Wheel, in which he considers there to be eight primary emotions. This activity enables EYPs and EYTs to use colours, pictures and words to support children to describe and understand their emotions better.

Figure 5.5 Example of an Emotion Wheel for children.

People can struggle with communicating how they feel; therefore, using clear emotion labels can help individual express their feelings, and have more awareness of their emotions and in turn communicate their needs.

Sit in a circle with a small group and introduce children to the Emotion Wheel using the prompt, 'I am feeling…'. Depending on the age of the children, you can ask each child to name and describe how they are feeling and either place their chosen emotion face on the 'Emotion Wheel', draw the emotion or point it out.

This encourages children to become more aware of and express their feelings in a safe and caring environment. With this information, adults can work daily to co-regulate and reassure children that it is okay to feel sad, worried, angry or tired and that we all feel a range of emotions.

This circle time activity encourages listening skills, turn-taking and enables children to express how they feel. They can draw or talk about their feelings as a follow-up activity, and adults can provide them with strategies to manage their feelings, such as sitting and noticing their breathing, sitting in a quiet area or going for a mindful walk.

Links to EYFS: Children will learn how to describe and name their emotions and show an understanding of their own feelings. They will show sensitivity to the feelings of others and through mindfulness techniques will learn ways to regulate their behaviour and emotions.

2. Garden safari

This activity encourages movement and is a fun way to help children practice mindfulness outdoors. It can be planned as a sensory activity with a small group of children in the outdoor area of your setting, a local park or a suitable natural environment in the local area.

Figure 5.6 **Nine boy faces with different emotions and example emotion wheel.**

Start by encouraging children to dress up in safari clothing and turn their daily walk or planned activity into an exciting safari adventure. Sit the children in a circle and ask them to listen out for different sounds around them. They can put up their hands to share the sounds they can hear. Next, show the children pictures and read a story about safari animals focussing on the facial features, sounds and colours of each animal.

The children then have time to explore the different areas of the safari that you have set up, giving them time to take pictures or draw the animals, bugs, animals and birds on the safari. EYPs and EYTs can use soft toy animals, cut-outs and pictures of a range of animals, birds and their babies for the safari experience.

Children will learn to focus all their senses using binoculars to hunt and find insects and animals in the outdoor environment. This activity is a mindful exploration using a safari theme with the opportunity to use trees, plants, a range of animals, labels and photos to create the ultimate safari experience. It will inspire curiosity and exploring the natural world.

Links to EYFS: Children will learn to be self-confident to try new activities and show independence, resilience and perseverance with the challenge of a mindful garden safari walk. Gross motor skills, language and communication skills will be developed.

3. Mindfulness bingo game

Table 5.1 shows a bingo card game that can be provided to support children's mindfulness.

Invite children to sit together indoors or outdoors to play this mindfulness bingo game, suitable for up to six children. Give them a mindfulness board each and counters. They take turns to choose and read the card statements, helping them to read the mindful task they will be doing. When complete they match it to the statement on their board. Continue until someone has completed a line horizontally, vertically or diagonally. For younger children you can use pictures and short phrases, with no more than four tasks on their board.

The 'mindfulness board' provided here can be adapted for the children in your setting. You can use this activity to encourage participation, listening skills, following

Table 5.1 **Bingo Game Card**

List or say five things you are grateful for	Find something hard, soft and smooth – describe them	Enjoy one minute sitting quietly, noticing any sounds around you
Stand and stretch, then go into tree pose and take three long breaths	Give someone a compliment	Listen to your favourite rhyme, song or music
Find a flower with a nice smell, sit and draw the flower	Take a mindful walk, feeling the grass under your feet	Eat a piece of fruit mindfully, notice how it tastes
Name two things you can hear	Draw a picture of your favourite animal	Take five deep breaths and do five shoulder rolls

rules and turn-taking as well as encouraging children to use their senses as they try out the mindful tasks.

Links to EYFS: Children will learn turn-taking skills, listening and working together in a group. They will be confident to try new activities, show sensitivity to others needs and feelings, play co-operatively, read simple sentences, improving language and vocabulary.

4. Mindful story time

Story time is an effective way to integrate mindfulness into your curriculum. There are many mindfulness books that encourage children to apply mindfulness into their day and be in the present moment. Sharing stories daily with children of all ages introduces mindfulness in a fun and relaxing way. This can be a one to one, small or large group activity and inviting children to the book area regularly further encourages children to enjoy looking at books, reading and listening to stories.

Choosing a book, turning the pages and absorbing themselves in the pictures and words can be a practical and effective daily mindful activity.

Equally, listening to a story read by adults fosters a stronger bond between the practitioner and children and will enable children to sit mindfully and tune into their senses as they enter a world of characters, plots and adventures that can cultivate present-moment awareness. You can introduce a range of books that are available in the setting, digital form with stories, rhymes and actions and encourage children to slow down, connect and use their imagination.

Links to EYFS: Recalling the story helps to talk about their own feelings and those of others and listen attentively and respond to what they hear. Books also enable children to develop cognitive skills in particular memory recall, thinking, concentration and being imaginative and expressive.

Here are four books to support children's mindfulness.

Table 5.2 provides a list of mindfulness story books for children.

Table 5.2 Mindfulness Story Books for Children

Title	Author
Today, We Have No Plans	Jan Godwin and Anna Walker
Bee Still	Frank Sileo and Claire Keay
My Majic Breath: Finding Calm Through Mindful Breathing	Nick Ortner, Alison Taylor and Michelle Polizzi
The Secret to Clara's Calm	Tamara Levitt

5. Mindful stretch and yoga

Introducing children to simple stretches and yoga poses can considerably improve their body strength, self-confidence and support stress reduction. Yoga is a great way to develop gross motor skills and support children's balance, co-ordination and focus. They learn to direct their energy positively with daily exercise and movement.

Yoga is suitable for babies and children and using a theme such as 'animal yoga' can be particularly fun and enjoyable for children and one of the best ways to engage them. They can be introduced to making shapes and holding postures to build physical strength and mental focus. EYPs and EYTs can introduce yoga as a morning routine in the setting, using an indoor or outdoor space.

From being a peaceful and calm butterfly to a strong and balanced downward dog, this activity can be shared with parents and families to do at home to build positive relationships. Making cards with pictures and instructions will provide endless fun and opportunities for children.

Table 5.3 lists a range of animal yoga poses with instructions for children.

Links to EYFS: Daily stretching and movement is a fun way to build large muscles and teach children to focus and follow specific instructions. They also learn to play co-operatively and develop confidence to try new activities.

The Early Years Foundation Stage

There are seven areas of learning and development that shape educational programmes in early years settings. These are divided into three prime areas and four specific areas.

Table 5.3   Animal Yoga Poses for Children

Animal yoga	Instructions
Butterfly pose	Sit on the floor and bring your feet together, placing one hand onto each ankle. Flutter the knees gently up and down floating the body from side to side, count five breaths.
Downward dog pose	Start in a table top position, tuck your toes under and lift hips up and back, stretching your arms, back and legs, count three breaths then lower down to table top.
Cat pose	Kneel on all fours like a cat, slowly arch your back and look down towards your tummy. Then lower your belly and lift your head to look forward, count three breaths and repeat.
Frog pose	Squat on the floor, balancing on your toes, knees out to the side, hands in front on the floor. Look up and breathe in, as you breathe out straighten your legs into a forward bend position, lowering your head. Lower down and repeat three times.
Cobra pose	Start on the belly, bring your hands flat to the ground under the shoulders and press up with your hands to lift your head and shoulders up. . Use

Personal, social and emotional development (PSED) is one of the three Prime areas within the EYFS. Each prime area is divided into early learning goals.

The early learning goals for PSED are:

- Self-regulation.

- Managing self.

- Building relationships.

The early learning goal statements for *Self-Regulation* that embrace mindfulness are:

Children at the expected level of development will:

Show an understanding of their own feelings and those of others and begin to regulate their behaviour accordingly.

Set and work towards simple goals, being able to wait for what they want and control their immediate impulses when appropriate.

Give focused attention to what the teacher says, responding appropriately even when engaged in activity.

The early learning goal statements for *Managing Self* that embrace mindfulness are:

Children at the expected level of development will:

Be confident to try new activities and show independence, resilience and perseverance in the face of challenge.

Explain the reasons for rules, know right from wrong and try to behave accordingly.

The early learning goal statements for *Building Relationships* that embrace mindfulness are:

Children at the expected level of development will:

Work and play cooperatively and take turns with others.

Form positive attachments to adults and friendships with peers.

Show sensitivity to their own and to others' needs.

(DfE, 2021, p. 12)

Reflective task

Work with your team to discuss and reflect upon how you currently plan for and support children's wellbeing and mental health in line with the EYFS early learning goals.

If you are in a leadership role, what processes or training are in place for staff to support children's mental health and wellbeing?

Study the image shown here and describe the value of this activity for children and how it supports their wellbeing.

Following discussion and reflection, the chances are that you are already providing opportunities for children to recognise and manage their feelings and express their emotions. The use of observations to assess children's needs, auditing the internal and external play environment and regular staff meetings help to reflect on creating mindful play opportunities for babies, toddlers and pre-school age children.

Please note: The mindfulness activities, practices and techniques selected for children in this chapter are based on ideas from my own early years practice and

Figure 5.7   **Boy and girl sitting in red cart.**

training programmes that I have accessed. They provide ideas for incorporating mindfulness into the curriculum and daily routine. You do not need to be trained in teaching mindfulness; however, you must have an awareness and understanding of what mindfulness is. This book provides the understanding required for EYPs and EYTs to model mindfulness and support development of children's ability to build relationships, manage-self and self-regulate.

15 Mindfulness activities for children

Here is a toolkit of 15 mindfulness activities that can be built into the curriculum for children in your setting.

In this section you will learn about a range of mindfulness activities that can be planned and implemented for children in your early years setting.

The activities are suitable for children across the age range from birth to 5 years.

When we think about mindfulness, we tend to associate it with being still or quiet. However, mindfulness also involves movement, therefore making it ideal for children as they like to move as part of their natural curiosity for learning.

These activities combine movement and mindfulness supported by adults and aim to provide enjoyment and engagement by everyone.

From reading chapter four you will have a better awareness of mindfulness and may have committed to your own daily practice using the ideas from the previous chapter. It is now time to think about how to introduce and teach some of these key principles of mindfulness to children in a way this is accessible, fun and explorative.

Activity one: Mindful breathing activities

Breathing activities with children are simple and effective mindfulness techniques that can be done at any time of the daily routine. 'Children benefit from focussing on their breathing when emotions are hard to manage' (Currid, 2020).

Breathing activity ideas

Table 5.4 provides some simple breathing techniques for children.

Belly breathing mindfulness activity (2–5 years old)

This breathing aims to support children to:

1. Notice how their body feels.

2. Follow the breath.

3. Say Hello to the mind and thoughts.

Table 5.4   Simple Breathing Techniques for Children

Picture or shape breathing	Activity cards with a picture or shape such as a square, star, rainbow or flower provide a useful visual resource to use with children.
	They can follow their breath along the outside of the picture or shape as they breathe in and out, helping them to feel calm and relaxed.
Shoulder roll breathing	Shoulder roll breaths help children to move the body and release any tension in the neck and shoulders.
	As they take a deep breath in, encourage them to roll their shoulders up toward their ears then drop their shoulders back down on the exhale.
Hot chocolate breathing	Encourage children to sit on the floor and model how to create a cup shape curling their fingers and placing one hand in front of the other.
	Ask them to imagine that inside the cup circle is some delicious hot chocolate. They can breathe in slowly to smell the hot chocolate and blow out carefully to cool their drink, repeating several times.

Figure 5.8 **Child sitting with legs crossed and eyes closed.**

Script to follow: How does your body feel today?

We are going to sit with our teddy/toy and rest our body.

Let's all sit in a space and close our eyes.

Now just breathe in through your nose and breathe out through your mouth. Well done!

Place your teddy onto your belly and lie down on the floor. Notice what happens to your teddy when you breathe in through your nose – let children respond. Now breathe out – what happens to your tummy?

Breathe in again and notice how your teddy lifts when your belly fills up with air, then as you breathe out your teddy rests down.

Did you notice your tummy going up and down?

How do you feel? Are you feeling happy, calm, relaxed?

Activity two: Blowing bubbles and balloon play (babies to 5 years old)

In the outdoor area, introduce children to blowing bubbles. If the children are younger or are babies, then adults can blow the bubbles. Encourage them to pay close attention to the bubbles and watch them float away.

Support children to pop the bubbles with their hands or stamp on them as they fall to the ground. This mindful activity encourages children to observe and notice what is happening in the present moment.

This can lead onto playing with balloons, where you can introduce a simple game of tapping the balloon and keeping it off the ground for older children. For babies, they can hold and let go of the balloon. Drawing faces on the balloons showing different expressions is a good way to introduce children to talk about their emotions.

Ask children how they feel during the activity and afterwards. Use picture cards for children to follow visual cues of body shapes, asking how does your body feel and how does your mind feel?

Finish by everyone joining hands to make a circle of nice tall trees, balancing on one leg, then lying on the floor in a circle to make a beautiful flower shape, stretching their arms and legs out wide, counting their breath from 1 through to 10.

Activity three: Yoga time (babies to 5 years old)

Yoga has many benefits and provides children with life skills in mindful movement and exercise. It can have a positive impact on children's wellbeing and give them the opportunity to learn how to improve concentration, body awareness, concentration and memory, whilst learning a range of postures in a fun and organic way.

One way for children to experience mindfulness naturally is through body postures and movements. Choose an open, quiet and familiar space for children

Figure 5.9 **Children in a class doing yoga.**

and remind them that doing these stretches, poses and movements will make them strong, happy and healthy. You can model the postures and ask children to:

- Stand tall and still like a mountain.
- Balance in tree pose.
- Sit in lotus pose.
- Lie on their belly in cobra pose.
- Become a warrior in warrior 1 and 2 pose.
- Forward fold pose.
- Boat pose.
- Bridge pose.

You can make picture cards showing each yoga pose to guide children.

Baby yoga can be carried out with a trained adult guiding staff in a small group indoors or outdoors. This is a simple and effective way to introduce babies to yoga movements supported by adults.

Activity four: Wellbeing wall or tree (1–5 years old)

Setting up a wellbeing wall or tree helps promotes what is positive in children's lives. This is a mindful way to encourage children to talk about what they enjoy doing, who they like and what makes them feel happy.

Initially, children can help to make the wall or tree as a 'go to' activity set up on the wall as a display, or a real tree or wall outdoors can work well too.

Children can be encouraged to make bricks and leaves from card or paper and then talk about what they are grateful for, who was kind to them, something they enjoyed learning or doing or children can draw how they feel or what they are grateful for today. The tree and the wall can grow with lots of new leaves and bricks each day, as children add to their wellbeing wall or tree. This can be shared with parents, carers and visitors to the nursery to highlight the importance of children expressing their feelings, thoughts and emotions and what they are grateful for.

Activity five: How does angry feel? (2–5 years old)

Anger is an emotion we all feel from time to time. How do you handle your own anger? Is it managed and then you move on, or does it affect you for hours or even days afterwards?

There will be moments in a day when some children will feel emotions that they cannot control or manage. When this happens, the support of the early years practitioner to step in with emotional support and help children to manage their feelings by first modelling effective strategies to calm the body and mind, such as taking a deep breath, counting or going for a walk. Then when appropriate empathise with children and reassure them that emotions can be positive and negative, modelling techniques.

Questions to ask children: Tell me how your body feels when you are angry?

My face feels _____, My eyes feels _____, My belly feels _____

Next time I feel angry I will _____

Figure 5.10   **Face of a boy showing the emotion 'anger'.**

A good emotional environment will 'provide a secure base from which children grow into well-rounded, capable adults with robust mental health' (DfE, 2003; Every Child Matters).

Figure 5.11 **Sun smiling.**

Activity six: Sunshine heart pose (babies to 5 years old)

Practice this simple moving activity with a child or group of children at the start of the day as part of the daily routine. Ask children to slowly raise their arms forward, then out to the side and then up to the sky.

Look up and reach for some sunshine. Hold this in your hand and bring it down to your heart centre. Pause, take a soft breath in through the nose and out through the mouth and relax. EYPs and EYTs can work one-on-one with babies to gently move their arms and help them stretch and move.

Children feel the air being pushed forwards, to the sides and upwards as they move their arms and hands. This silences the mind and helps them to feel calm and relaxed.

Activity seven: Create a calm cave or calm corner (1–5 years old)

Setting up a calm cave or calm corner provides children with a designated space in the setting with the intent of providing them with a safe space to go to when they feel their emotions are running too high, or if they need quiet time to feel calm and regain their emotional wellbeing.

Encourage children to create a calm cave and setting it up with all their favourite quiet things that they like to do.

You can include calming music, blankets, yoga mats and enable children to create their calm place to sit and enjoy quiet time. As well as moving around and exploring their environment, children can incorporate mindful moments into their day with an area that invites them to sit and be.

Figure 5.12 **Two children lying down in opposite directions.**

Activity eight: Just one breath (2–5 years old)

Many children enjoy sitting and noticing their breath. Just one breath is a simple breathing activity that you can do with a small or large group of children.

a. Find a relaxing and familiar place to sit comfortably, with cushions or a large mat, indoors or outdoors.

b. Set a timer for one minute and ask the children to close their eyes and really listen to any sounds that they can hear.

c. Ask them to take a big breath in through their nose and out from their mouth and notice how they feel.

d. Then ask them to take another slow deep breath, imagining the air going into their belly filling up like a balloon. Then breathing all the air from their belly by blowing out of their mouth, squeezing all the air out of the balloon.

Activity nine: Wellbeing questionnaire (babies to 5 years old)

■ This activity enables EYPs and EYTs to work with parents and carers to learn about the uniqueness of their child, including their likes, dislikes, needs and interests. The 'Wellbeing Questionnaire' forms a second step to the 'All About Me' form.

■ **All About Me** forms are a traditional part of the transition process in getting to know a child when they start at the setting. You may have a template that you already use in your setting.

■ **The Wellbeing Questionnaire** provides a mindful way for settings to support children to learn more about themselves and can include a range of questions and activities for children to do at the setting or at home to enhance their wellbeing. This activity supports working positively in partnership with parents and families to complete a wellbeing review and make plans for improvements and next steps for children's wellbeing.

Sample Wellbeing Questionnaire

I like to:	My favourite activities are:	I don't like:
What makes me feel happy at nursery:	What makes me feel happy at home:	
Does anything make me sad or upset sometimes:		
Healthy food that is good for my body:	My favourite food is:	Unhealthy food that is not so good for my body:
Today I felt some of these emotions and feelings: Happy ____Grateful_____ Excited____ Sad____ Tired_____Angry 😊 What made me feel this way:		
My friend at nursery are:		
Things I like to do that keep me fit and active: (Tell me or draw a picture)		
Achievements ⭐		
Who helps me learn and achieve the things I want?	What am I learning to do and getting better at?	Something I have achieved and can do well is:

Activity ten: Texture feely bag (3–5 years old)

Put a selection of objects with different shapes, sizes and textures into a cloth bag. Ask the children to sit in a circle and take turns to and reach into the bag and feel one of the objects, without looking at it. They learn to use their sense of touch to feel the object and then describe the shape, texture and properties of the objects using as much detail as possible. This mindful activity enables children to explore a range of objects and materials and supports their language and communication skills too.

Activity eleven: Qi Gong movement (3–5 years old)

Mindful movement each day helps children to move their body with more awareness. One important reason for this is that in daily life children are mostly moving and rarely still, and mindfulness is not just about sitting still. So helping children learn mindful movements helps them to be mindful in everyday activities, such as waiting to wash their hands, when eating or going for a walk.

Figure 5.13   **Two girls standing with white t-shirt and red shorts.**

To start with, ask the children to let their body go loose and floppy to music, then start to lengthen and stand tall like statues. They can place their hands on the belly and bringing them out to the side slowly, returning to the belly on the exhale making a tree shape, and repeating. Next, twisting the body round from side to side, gently swinging the arms and breathing in and breathing out. Remind them, if the mind wanders, they can simply bring it back to their breathing. Lastly, ask children to do a wake-up stretch, so start with the hands on the belly, breathing in and then stretching the arms up on the exhale, really enjoying that feeling of letting go and relaxing as the arms go up and then back down to the belly. Repeat at least five times, making a circle as the arms stretch up and down.

Activity twelve: Glitter bottle (babies to 5 years old)

Babies and young children use their senses to learn about the world around them. If babies appear upset or need to be soothed, a glitter bottle provides a visual distraction to help them gain attention and focus on the swirling glitter in a bottle of water.

With children 3–5 years, ask them to think of themselves as a glitter bottle. The glitter and water in the bottle is their mind and the bottle is their body. Ask them what happens to the glitter when you move and shake the bottle? Affirm that the water becomes very busy and the glitter swirls around, but if we allow the bottle to be still, then what happens to the glitter in the water?

The children will notice how the glitter settles and the water becomes clear. Tell them that the same is true when we sit mindfully our mind becomes clearer and more still. If we keep moving our body a lot, our mind doesn't get the chance to settle.

This activity encourages children to sit still and notice their body and mind.

Activity Thirteen: Moving with awareness (babies to 5 years old)

The more you embed mindfulness into the daily routine, the easier it is to engage children. You can use this short script to support children's focus, attention and listening skills (adapted: Cowan, 2010).

Start with some mindful movements:

- Aim to get children to stand still and breathe … how does that feel?

- Next try to get children to walk around on their toes, with their shoulders hunched up, hopping, taking big steps, taking small steps, with a smile on their face, walking slow, walking fast … how does that feel?

- Encourage them to tap into their feelings as they move with more body awareness

Figure 5.14   **Girl with butterfly wings.**

Say to the children: 'We are going to sit/stand in our mindful bodies and take a deep breath in, then a deep breath out'.

'Now we will sit/stand with our backs tall and eyes closed. Listen and place you attention on the sound you are about to hear'.

Choose a soft sound such as a bell, piece of music, musical instrument such as a triangle or a rainstick.

'Listen until the sound is completely gone'. Repeat the sound and encourage children to sit and listen one more time.

'Raise your hand when you can no longer hear the sound'

'Please raise your hand when you can no longer hear the sound'.

When most or all have raised their hands, you can say, *'Now slowly, mindfully, move your hand to your stomach or chest, and just feel your breathing'.*

You can help students stay focused during the breathing with reminders like, *'Just breathing in … just breathing out …'*

Activity fourteen: Mindful eating (babies to 5 years old)

Mindful eating encourages children to use their senses and to practice eating using small 'mindful bites' to taste the food and notice the textures and flavours. Mealtimes and snack times help children to enhance their social skills and independence in feeding themselves or being supported by adults. Mindful eating helps children focus on the present and slow down when eating, to recognise feelings of hunger and fullness.

A simple activity such as food tasting enables children to use the five senses and learn about each food in a relaxed and calm environment. By modelling mindful eating, you can encourage children to remain present by drawing upon their senses to smell, taste, chew and enjoy the food. You can give children a selection of fruits and vegetables, considering any allergies that they may have.

Start by encouraging children to look at the food and notice the shape and colour, asking them if it is soft, hard or crunchy. Ask them to chew it slowly and describe how it tastes. Is it sweet, salty, juicy and how does it smell?

Question prompts to engage the five senses and enable mindful eating are:

See: What does it look like? What colour is it? What shape is it?

Touch: What does it feel like? Is it soft or hard? Is it smooth or rough?

Taste: How does it taste? Is it sweet or salty? Is it a good or bad taste?

Listen: What sounds do you hear when you eat the food?

Smell: How does it smell? Is it a nice smell? Describe the smell?

Figure 5.15   Girl sitting on a book floating in sky.

Activity fifteen: Colours in nature

Colouring is an activity that can be therapeutic and relaxing for many children. They may make patterns and pictures or colour in from print outs provided for them by adults. To extend colouring into the outdoors, after a mindful walk gathering and finding natural objects to draw and colour, introduce children to painting and using resources such as oil pastels to colour and paint leaves, wooden logs, flowers, acorns, sticks and stones. Children can get involved in the natural textures and lines of these objects. For example the painted leaf below can be displayed on the mindful wall. Additionally, children can create collages and mandalas using the materials.

Planning mindfulness activities for the prime areas of learning

This section provides a guide to planning and developing a whole setting approach to mindfulness as a tool in developing a wellbeing approach in your early years setting. You can implement simple changes to gain real benefit and bring awareness of mindful activities that bring focus, calm and enjoyment in each day.

- The activities are linked to the prime areas of learning within the early years foundation stage (EYFS) for the birth to five age range.

- When planning for children's learning and development you can incorporate activities provided in this chapter, as well as activities and techniques from your own research, knowledge and experience.

Figure 5.16 **Six children cartoons standing.**

Planning for mindfulness in your early years setting

Table 5.5 provides a range of mindfulness activities that can be offered to children to support the three prime areas of learning of the Early Years Foundation Stage (EYFS).

Table 5.5   Range of Mindfulness Activities for Children Supporting the Prime Areas of Learning

Prime area of learning and development	Babies (birth to 20 months)	Toddlers (16–36 months)	Pre-school (36–60 months)
Physical development	Explore treasure baskets; empty and fill material boxes; mirrors and reflections; music and instruments for movement; food tasting; sensory play; baby yoga guided; mark making with paint; eating snacks; exploring indoor and outdoor spaces to encourage free movement, rolling and stretching; explore sounds and sights; discovery bottles; bubble play	Make playdough; explore a range of textures and malleable materials; obstacle course; pouring and filling containers with water and sand; feeding themselves; rest and sleep opportunities; movement games with cones, beanbags and hoops; blowing bubbles Construction play; easel painting and drawing; yoga, stretching, movement	Cooking, painting, singing activities with actions; range of tools for cutting, creating and design work; construction equipment and writing tools; outdoor opportunities to walk, run, cycle, build; free movement and exploration of spaces; animal yoga; team games; action rhymes and stories; rest times; forest school activities; dance and mindful movement; listening walk; planting and digging
Personal, social and emotional development	Support transitions; one-to-one time; sitting alongside others, sharing toys; explore sensory toys, being attentive; share and reflect with parents; respond to interests; follow their lead; share familiar rhymes,	Encourage playing alongside others; co-operative games with familiar adults; encourage child-led play to build self-confidence; encourage making choices; create stories exploring feelings of the characters; talk about	Space and time to work together; share ideas; turn-taking activities; making choices, expressing preferences; sharing and talking about what they did and how they felt; share thoughts and feelings; use personal dolls to

(Continued)

Table 5.5   **Range of Mindfulness Activities for Children Supporting the Prime Areas of Learning (*Continued*)**

Prime area of learning and development	Babies (birth to 20 months)	Toddlers (16–36 months)	Pre-school (36–60 months)
	words, objects from home; cosy and quiet spaces to be calm; books reflecting feelings, comfort objects from home; free play activities that encourage spontaneity; watching clouds; mindful mealtimes	sharing, modelling this; share learning with parents; support children to manage their feelings; areas for rest and quiet time; role play area into a yoga class; mindful cave for relaxation; meditation music	help consider feelings; range of music to capture different moods; rest periods to support wellbeing; use pictures to show children expected behaviours; gratitude tree
Communication and language	Use key words in home language; singing new and familiar rhymes; follow children's lead, repeating sounds and words; commentary to support understanding during play, e.g. 'clap our hands, 1, 2,3'; short stories to read aloud; puppets, materials and objects that can be explored; listening to others; repeating sounds	Choose and share favourite books; role play to develop language; display pictures and talk about objects, and events; welcome, check feelings and emotions; listen and respond to news; ask questions to encourage speaking; allow time for responses; creating stories and narratives; listening ears; mindful walk	Story time and circle games indoors and outdoors; audio visualisations; picture story boards created with children; learning new songs and repeating; role play and drama; group reading; describing events, activities and feelings; sharing and reading books; learning sounds, words and developing written and spoken language

The role of the adult

The role of EYPs and EYTs is to support and promote the learning and development of children through play, so that they reach their full potential within a nurturing and supportive environment. Article 31 of the United Nations Convention on the Rights of the Child (UNCRC, 2016) states that 'Children have the right to relax and play, and to join in a wide range of cultural, artistic and other recreational activities'. Therefore, as professionals working with children, it is important to consider:

■ That all play activities are appropriate to the age and stage of development of the child. The role of the EY teachers and practitioners is to facilitate children's learning and development through modelling mindfulness.

■ The Key Person assigned to the child understands the role of mindfulness and takes the initiative to build a positive relationship with the child to create connections with parents and the home environment.

Activity

Now that you have a better understanding of the importance of planning mindfulness activities for children, you can start by planning a monthly calendar of mindfulness activities to form an effective 'toolkit' for your setting (see example provided in Table 5.6). This can be drawn upon and implemented alongside your weekly, termly and long-term planning.

The main aim of this task is to include fun, simple and effective mindfulness opportunities for children. Remember that mindfulness teaches children to observe their emotions as they arise and to encourage them to acknowledge their emotions without judgment, allowing them to pass.

Table 5.6   **Monthly Calendar of Mindfulness Activities for Children**

MONTH: _____				
Monday	*Tuesday*	*Wednesday*	*Thursday*	*Friday*
Tummy breathing with soft toy on belly	Look at a flower, close your eyes, visualise and draw it	Close your eyes and listen. What do you hear?	Try out a new healthy recipe – eat mindfully	Three things that make you happy
Worry tree – tell the tree your worries	Listen to a story, relax and enjoy	Move slowly around the garden	One minute body scan lying on the floor	Mindful colouring

Note: This calendar includes some activities to get you started.

For mindfulness and emotional learning to be effective, children require supportive and knowledgeable adults who can empathise and co-regulate with them. This happens when a child and adult adapt to each other's emotions and forms one of the foundations of the key person approach (Grenier, 2021). The important thing to remember is to support each child according to their needs, particularly when a child is struggling to manage overwhelming emotions which can affect their behaviour and mood. By being sympathetic and calm, children learn that their emotions and feelings can be managed through mindfulness techniques such as a positive visualisation, working with their feelings or physical play also associated with cognitive self-regulation.

The ability to self-regulate and manage a range of emotions gives children self-confidence in their daily life to manage different social contexts that they may encounter, preparing them from a young age to express their thoughts and feelings.

Therefore, the skills that adult's model and share with children build the essential foundations that can be developed throughout childhood into adulthood.

Five key strategies for an emotionally healthy early years setting

These strategies aim to ensure that all children are given equal opportunities to participate fully in your setting educational programme, to promote wellbeing and mental health. These strategies align with the EYFS framework to ensure that children learn and develop well.

1. **The first strategy is to know the children that you work with** by carrying out regular observations to identify their needs and interests. Review and reflect on your observations with others and then identify clear next steps to progress the learning and development of each child, evidencing this in your planning. Which areas will you focus on and why? If you note any concerns, then how will you address these? Next plan the learning environment by looking at it objectively; have a good knowledge of each child's interests and follow their lead; assess the space and then brainstorm creative ideas, experiences and activities that you can resource to support their learning and development. Children need a caring, stimulating and playful environment which is both safe and secure where they can be happy and valued as individuals. When entering your room and play based learning environment, does it enable play opportunities that are age appropriate and can be accessible by the children? Continually reviewing and adapting your planning to suit the children is a key aspect of providing a quality provision.

2. **The second strategy is to carry out a consistent 'plan, do and review' approach** to enable you to evaluate the impact of the setting's provision and

teaching methods on learning. For example, build on what children know and can already do, providing planned and purposeful experiences that support opportunities for children to engage in activities planned around their interests by adults and initiated themselves. Ensure that all children feel included, valued and are acknowledged as individuals, giving them time to express their needs from the moment they enter the setting. Develop systems to assess, track and monitor that they are progressing well within all areas of learning. Create a welcoming approach, learning key words used from a child's home language if English is an additional language. This will foster a sense of belonging. Also, consider if home languages of children are reflected in the displays, resources and daily talking points during the day.

3. **The third strategy is to take a positive approach** to ensure to ensure that all children feel included, secure and valued. It is crucial to build positive relationships with parents for you to work with them and to support their child's learning and growth. Early years experiences should build on what children already know and no child should be excluded or disadvantaged with the home and setting working together to achieve a common goal. Identify and note children's achievements clearly to form a purposeful learning journey and continue to identify next steps to extend learning. For example, if a child shows an interest in mealtimes and trying out different food tastes, you can plan a walk to the local shops to buy a range of healthy foods. The children can make a healthy fruit salad, and this can be followed up with a food tasting activity using a range of fruits and vegetables.

4. **The fourth strategy is starting with the end in mind** as an effective and forward-thinking approach to creating and achieving a holistic, playful and meaningful learning experience for all children. The passion and willingness of each early year's teacher and teacher to observe, assess and support learning regularly is a crucial starting point for making a difference to the wellbeing, learning and development of every child within the setting. This should incorporate understanding of and consideration of children's unique interests, strengths, stage of development, achievements and emotional needs during the daily routine. An awareness of the potential of the environment, how to organise it and the ability to reflect and improve will enable EYPs and EYTs to create purposeful opportunities for play and learning. Using play as a medium to support learning, it is important to acknowledge the interactions, relationship forming and interventions that play opportunities create (Moyles, 2010).

5. **The fifth strategy is sharing ideas** and creating a setting philosophy that underpins a wellbeing pedagogy is highly dependent upon a staff team that are passionate and motivated to support children's mental health and encourage children to form relationships, express their feelings and manage conflict through self-regulating. Additionally, giving children time to adapt to changes and encouraging

listening and opportunities to express and manage thoughts, feelings and emotions. Giving children a balanced and nutritional diet and regular physical play activities supports their physical and mental health.

The role of EYPs and EYTs is to fundamentally support children, and maximise learning opportunities by creating a play environment that enables creativity, originality and self-expression. A play-based curriculum sets the platform for providing an educational programme that supports the holistic learning and development of children. Facilitating learning and development opportunities requires careful planning, creative thinking and implementing with a good understanding of the benefits to children's development and wellbeing.

Conclusion

The role of mindfulness in early years continues to grow as an approach for enhancing the wellbeing of children and supporting their self-regulation skills.

This chapter has discussed the relevance of mindfulness within the EYFS and sets out mindfulness activities and strategies that can be adapted and implemented within your daily routines. A play-based mindfulness curriculum created by knowledgeable and skilled adults enables children to experience mindfulness as part of their learning opportunities within early years settings.

An important point to remember is to start from the children's needs, interests and curiosities to support and enable effective mindful learning opportunities to build the foundations of an emotionally healthy early years setting. This can be achieved by developing a whole setting approach and implementing a range of purposeful mindfulness activities within the daily routine for all children will support self-regulation skills. Mindfulness in the early year's curriculum aligns with the EYFS early learning goals and the government's agenda to enhance wellbeing for children.

The chapter provides the benefits of implementing mindfulness-based activities for children in their setting, discussing how this can be done in a fun, practical and creative way to support children's learning and development. This chapter provides a starting point for understanding and applying mindfulness within the daily routine. Activities can be carried out with children individually or in groups and fully support the prime areas of learning within the EYFS. The important role of the adult remains to support children's self-regulation skills with suggestions for engaging all children across the birth to five years. Finally, the chapter enables EYPs and EYTs to develop an understanding about the value of mindfulness and to create a toolkit of ideas when planning a balanced curriculum with wellbeing of children at its core.

References

Ackerman, C. (2022) *Positive Psychology: 25 Fund Mindfulness Activities for Children and Teens.* Accessed 29 March 2022 at https://positivepsychology.com/mindfulness-for-children-kids-activities/

Currid, J. (2020) *Mindfulness in Early Learning and Care.* Accessed on 12 June 2021 at https://knowledge.barnardos.ie/handle/20.500.13085/189

Department for Education (DfE) (2021) *Statutory Framework for the Early Years Foundation Stage. Setting the Standards for Learning, Development and Care for Children from Birth to Five.* Accessed on 12 December 2022 at https://assets.publishing.service.gov.uk/government/uploads/system/uploads/attachment_data/file/974907/EYFS_framework_-_March_2021.pdf

Department for Education (DfE) (Feb 2022) *State of the Nation 2021: Children and young people's wellbeing Research report* February. Accessed on 23 March 2022 at https://assets.publishing.service.gov.uk/government/uploads/system/uploads/attachment_data/file/1052920/SoN_2021-_executive_summary_220204.pdf

Gill, K. (2020) *Teaching Your Child Mindfulness.* Accessed on 26 July 2022 at https://www.healthline.com/health/childrens-health/mindfulness-for-kids

Grenier, J. (2021) Nursery World. EYFS guidance: effective practice. Focus points.

Holt, S., Atkinson, C. and Douglas-Osborn, E. (2022) *Exploring the Implementation of Mindfulness Approaches in an Early Years Setting. Journal of Early Childhood Research*, 20(2), pp. 214–228. Accessed on 19 April 2022 at https://doi.org/10.1177/1476718X211052790

Hölzel, B.K., Carmody, J., Vangel, M., Congleton, C., Yerramsetti, S.M., Gard, T. and Lazar, S.W. (2011) 'Mindfulness Practice Leads to Increases in Regional Brain Gray Matter Density', *Psychiatry Research*, 191(1), pp. 36–43. https://doi.org/10.1016/j.pscychresns.2010.08.006

Mindfulness in Schools Project (MISP) (2022) dots Curriculum (age 3 to 6). Accessed on 3 June 2022 at https://mindfulnessinschools.org/teach-dots-3-6/dots-curriculum-ages-3-6/

Moyles, J. (2010) *The Excellence of Play.* 3rd Edition. Open University Press. Maidenhead

Nieminen, S. and Sajaniemi, N. (2016) *Mindfulness Awareness in Early Childhood Education. South African Journal of Childhood Education*, ISSN: (Online) 2223-7682, (Print), pp. 2223–7674. Accessed on 14 May 2022 at https://files.eric.ed.gov/fulltext/EJ1187099.pdf and https://www.researchgate.net/publication/306921632_Mindful_awareness_in_early_childhood_education

6 The future of mindfulness in early years

Aims of Chapter 6

This chapter aims to:

- Summarise the effectiveness of introducing mindfulness into early years.
- Identify the cornerstones and benefits of mindfulness in the work environment.
- Provide a final case study to support the positive impact of mindfulness in practice.
- Discuss the future vision of mindfulness to enhance children's health and wellbeing.

Introduction

This book has set out to raise awareness about the importance of developing successful and effective mindfulness practices in early years settings. This final chapter highlights why mindfulness is important in the early years than ever before. It reaffirms the benefits to children's wellbeing and mental health, and the effectiveness of the three cornerstones to support the development of a successful mindfulness practice in your early years setting, and developing a whole setting approach to wellbeing.

The chapter highlights the value of mindfulness for both staff and children as an encouraging innovation to future-proof early years settings to prioritise wellbeing and tackle increasing mental health in young children. The chapter provides a final opportunity to practice mindful meditation and fully embrace the future vision of mindfulness in the early years, with a case study evaluating the impact of a mindfulness training programme for teachers.

DOI: 10.4324/9780429030734-7

Why is mindfulness important in the early years?

Following the pandemic, we continue to adapt to a busy and sometimes chaotic. As adults take on the challenges of work pressures, parenting and financial challenges, they strive to provide stability and balance in everyday family life. Children feel these stressors, and these challenges can become stressful and difficult to manage in the early years.

Mindfulness provides tools for children and encourages parents, practitioners, teachers and professionals to support children to develop healthy coping mechanisms to improve focus, attention and self-regulation and reduce stressors.

This book has identified mindfulness research studies, tools, strategies and models that can be incorporated to promote and develop a whole-setting approach to well-being through mindfulness as part of the curriculum.

The tools provided in this book can be used in a variety of ways to enable settings to evaluate and plan mindfulness provision to meet children's needs, particularly in the area of personal, social and emotional development. Through modelling practice, children will learn mindfulness techniques from knowledgeable early years practitioners (EYPs) and early years teachers (EYTs) in as little as a few minutes throughout the day. The most important thing to do is to 'get started' today with one activity from the book to start to promote mindfulness for children in your early years setting. Good luck!

Developing a successful mindfulness practice in your early years setting

Within the last two years, the early years sector has worked tirelessly to adapt policies, procedures and practices in line with pandemic and post-pandemic practices and regulations. As discussed in previous chapters, all settings can start a conversation to learn about the benefits of mindfulness by *applying these strategies*:

■ Using the mindfulness toolkits for children and staff provided in Chapters 4 and 5 to assess interest and understanding, enable staff to explore mindfulness for themselves as well as for planning and implementing activities and techniques with children, parents, colleagues and other settings.

■ Reading this book and referring to the suggested resources at the end of this chapter to learn more about the case for introducing mindfulness techniques into your workplace and to ensure there is understanding and an authentic mindfulness culture being developed.

■ Discover for yourself how mindfulness impacts your own wellbeing and capacity to be present and attuned to the needs of other staff, children, families and professionals. This aspect can be further supported by the case studies of individuals provided in this book, sharing the value of beginning their mindfulness journey.

These strategies can provide settings with a more robust and balanced daily routine and curriculum to support the wellbeing of children and staff now and in the future.

In applying the contents of this book, chapters 1, 2 and 3 begin to set the foundation blocks for mindfulness in your early year's setting. The remaining chapters 4, 5 and 6 help to create the social and emotional environment, thus enabling settings to plan and implement mindfulness into the daily routine.

To further support the development of mindfulness in your early years setting, the three cornerstones here provide a robust foundation for a successful daily mindful early year's practice.

Cornerstone one: Building **awareness** of slowing down and creating more experiences for stillness in the day – in practice, finding a place where children can sit and notice their thoughts, feeling and what is going on around them.

Cornerstone two: A positive **attitude** and commitment of self-practice from staff to create a mindful work environment – in practice, daily mindfulness activities and techniques for inner calm.

Cornerstone three: Embedding mindfulness within the setting tapestry to develop an **organisational culture** that supports social and emotional wellbeing for staff, children and families.

The most fundamental role of early years settings is to maintain consistency and continually assess the interest and relevance of mindfulness within the daily routine and curriculum. This can be achieved through thoughtful planning of the early year's curriculum, nurturing a staff team that focuses on being responsive adults, able to co-regulate with children in a calm and attentive manner. The goal is to support the development of happy and positive relationships and help children realise their potential in all areas of development, particularly emotional wellbeing.

As a setting, the importance of success is to discuss and reflect on the impact of mindfulness in daily conversations, at team meetings and during training. In time this will lead to an increased recognition of the positive impact on the mental health of those working with children and the development of children's emotional wellbeing.

A movement towards a wellbeing curriculum can, in turn, lead to positive changes within the sector as more and more settings provide mindfulness training and tools for their staff. Additionally, a growing number of settings have adopted a wellbeing policy and processes to support and enhance the mental and emotional health of their staff teams. There is a sample Mental Health and Wellbeing policy in the appendices and a sample Early Years Curriculum Plan.

The Chartered Institute of Personnel and Development (CIPD) identify the importance of fostering employee wellbeing as a positive for both the individual and the organisation. They emphasise that 'promoting wellbeing can help prevent stress and create positive working environment where individuals and organisations can thrive' (CIPD, 2021).

Wellbeing remains a focus for the government and the early years sector with reports such as the Preschool Learning Alliance Report (2018) highlighting that a

Figure 6.1   **Boy sitting in a field.**

high proportion of nursery workers and childminders commented on experiencing stress, anxiety and depression as a result of their work. The survey also revealed that 57% of the early years workforce reported on suffering from anxiety as a result of their work, and 26% experiencing depression.

Alongside this, a report by Mind (2019) identifies that 'good staff wellbeing is essential for cultivating a mentally healthy school, for retaining and motivating staff and for promoting pupil wellbeing and attainment'. A more recent survey in which approximately 1500 nursery staff participated, was published by the Anna Freud Centre (2021). Some of the key findings highlight that staff stress levels and mental health due to the pandemic have impacted on their wellbeing. The survey also found that although nursery staff enjoy their work, almost half were not aware of there being a staff mental health and wellbeing policy in place. The sample policy provided is a good starting point for settings to ensure that mental health and wellbeing are at the forefront of supporting early years staff in their work environments.

The importance of supporting children's emotional wellbeing and self-regulation is becoming a more prominent area within educational settings as part of the Early Years Foundation Stage framework and guidance. The Ofsted inspection framework and government initiatives to improve outcomes for all children remain at the forefront of early years practice. In contrast, when it comes to the emotional wellbeing of staff, the survey highlights that although early years staff 'love their work … it can at times be emotionally demanding and stressful' (Album, 2021). Therefore, appropriate interventions and wellbeing initiatives can provide mechanisms of support to ensure that staff wellbeing is a focus for employers.

When there are good levels of wellbeing in the workplace, this can improve not only absenteeism but better mental health among staff. The Department of Health (2014) support the notion that 'wellbeing has been found to have an impact on many aspects of people's lives such as their health, work and social relationships'. Therefore, appropriate support and early interventions could raise levels of staff wellbeing with commitment of heads and managers reviewing and prioritising wellbeing and mental health at work policies and procedures for staff.

The World Happiness Report (2019) is a national survey measuring the global state of happiness across 156 countries to identify the world's happiest countries. The UK ranked fifth and has remained in this ranking position for several years now with a focus on factors including technologies, social norms, government policies, life expectancy, freedom and *wellbeing*. Finland has been ranked the happiest country in the world once again.

When considering the wellbeing and happiness of your staff, a useful activity to assess current happiness levels in a subjective way is to try this activity and then relate it to work if needed to start discussions about creating a happier work environment for staff and children.

Happiness activity: What does happiness look like for you?

■ Think of the word happiness and the feeling of being happy. Would it be a person, object, memory, an experience? Or is it something more internal or abstract?

■ Try holding the image or idea of happiness in your mind, and all that you associate with it.

■ Now create a drawing or describe it here. Remember that what makes us happy can change day to day, so think of one thing that represents 'happy' for you at this moment.

Future proof early years settings with mindfulness

Mindfulness can help us in many ways, in particular understanding our emotions and managing our thoughts and feelings. It enables us to:

■ Feel calmer in our body and mind and less overwhelmed

■ Be more focused and present at the moment

■ Improve our attention and concentration with daily task

■ Manage our difficult thoughts and regulate emotions

Mindfulness approaches can significantly reduce symptoms of anxiety and depression and improve our wellbeing. The Mindful Nation UK Report (Mindfulness All Party Group (MAPPG), 2015) provides further information about the value of mindfulness-based approaches and case studies to support the value of mindfulness. The link to this report is available in the appendices.

Mindfulness training for education settings is an investment in reducing the costs of absenteeism which can be associated with stress-related conditions, as well as improving employee retention, satisfaction, and overall engagement. To reiterate, mindfulness is a simple yet powerful practice of training our attention and focus to the present moment and has been shown to be very effective in reducing stress and anxiety. It is defined as 'paying attention to thoughts and feelings without trying to distinguish whether they are right or wrong' (Kinsner et al., 2018).

Staff learn to proactively manage their state of mind and employers benefit with:

■ Reduced costs of staff absenteeism and lower turnover

■ Increased concentration, memory and learning skills

■ Increased productivity

■ Greater resilience in recovering from negative mental states

■ Enhanced job satisfaction

■ Enhanced employer/employee and client relationships

Benefits of mindfulness at work

Just to recap, here are some of the key benefits of mindfulness:

■ Incorporating mindfulness activities into daily life within the work setting can be simple and cost-effective for settings.

■ Most activities can be selected by individuals and implemented during the daily routine with children, in a small group or on your own, so both children and adults benefit.

■ When we practice mindfulness regularly, it can reduce stress levels, enhance performance and clarity of mind and increase attention.

Essentially mindfulness in early years settings can help us to pause, notice what is going on around us and reset with self-awareness and non-judgment. Subsequently, the mind becomes calmer and less cluttered with thoughts, and we learn to approach our experiences with more compassion, warmth and understanding.

Ultimately, it is about practising the skill of gently directing the mind to the present moment. 'Anyone who wants to improve their day-to-day wellbeing can practice mindfulness. While it has roots in Buddhism, you don't have to be religious or spiritual to practice" (Mental Health Foundation, 2021).

The good news is that with some planning and forethought, almost everything can be done mindfully. *The mindfulness activities in this book will offer you the opportunity to practice slowing down and becoming more aware of your thoughts, feelings and surroundings.* Creating a well-planned social and emotional environment can contribute to supporting children's 'confidence, wellbeing and self-awareness' (Mukadam and Sutherland, 2018).

People who regularly implement mindfulness strategies may find lasting physical and psychological benefits including:

- Increased experience of calm and relaxation

- Higher levels of energy and enthusiasm for living

- Increased self-confidence and self-acceptance

- Less danger of experiencing stress, depression, anxiety, chronic pain, addiction or low immune efficiency

- More self-compassion and compassion for others and our planet

(Dr. Collard, 2014)

Mindfulness can be utilised as a technique to reduce and manage stress, empowering employees in the workplace to manage their feelings and emotions using a range of techniques that bring present moment awareness, calm and relaxation. This, in turn, leads to better productivity and the ability to reset your mind to think in a healthier, less stressful way.

Mindfulness and meditation

Mindfulness is available to us in every moment as this book has affirmed. We can also be mindful through **meditations**, body scans and simple practices like taking time to pause and breathe or gentle movements and stretching to calm and relax the body.

Put simply, meditation is simply exploring your mind, emotions and thoughts through a guided means or by zoning into your inner self with kindness and compassion to ourselves and others.

Through meditation we practice and cultivate mindfulness with the intent to build awareness of the present moment. Therefore, meditation can be defined as 'a set of techniques that are intended to encourage a heightened state of awareness and focused attention. Meditation is also a consciousness-changing technique that has been shown to have a wide number of benefits on psychological well-being' (Cherry, 2020).

Mindfulness Meditation Activity

Figure 6.2   **Lady sitting in mediation.**

1. Sit comfortably on the floor, on a mat, cushion or chair. Whatever you choose to sit on, find a position that is comfortable for you.

2. Notice how you are sitting and lengthen your spine – but don't stiffen your upper body. Your head and neck can rest comfortably on top.

3. Place your arms and hands onto your thighs and either cross your legs if seated on the floor, or place both your feet onto the floor if seated on a chair.

4. Drop your chin and allow your gaze to fall downwards, closing your eyes if comfortable.

5. Sit here for a few moments and relax, bringing your attention to your breath and notice sensations in your body.

6. Then all you do for the next few minutes is to notice your breathing, following the inhale and exhale. Try to leave a pause after the inbreath and put more emphasis and length on the outbreath.

7. You may find your mind wandering constantly as you sit and breathe. This is normal, so just notice your thoughts without reacting to them. If your mind wanders repeatedly, come back to your breathing without judgment.

8. Continue to follow your breath for a few minutes, and when you are ready, gently lift your gaze or open your eyes.

9. Notice how your body feels, check in and notice your thoughts and emotions. Appreciate this pause in your day as a calming way to reset.

10. Finally, choose to continue your day more mindfully, with more awareness and attention of what is happening moment by moment.

Remember that you can choose to play gentle music when doing your mindful mediation. Alternatively, you can use an App such as 'Calm' or 'Headspace' to help you settle into a comfortable position for a mindful meditation each day, whenever feels right for you.

A mindful meditation practice is about finding a place to sit where you will have some quiet time for yourself, then paying attention to your breath. When your mind wanders during the guided practice, which may include music or a narration, simply return to your breath.

The future vision of mindfulness

We are undoubtedly living in challenging times with the pandemic raising the importance of protecting and supporting children's health and wellbeing. Many EYPs, EYTs and all adults working with children make a huge difference by incorporating techniques such as mindfulness to support children's mental health and develop those all-important self-regulation skills.

By encouraging children to focus on their breathing provides them with a simple technique to remain in the present moment. The simple concept of mindfulness has continued to develop in popularity and emerge successful in a study conducted by Saltzman at Stanford University, which showed decreases in anxiety and improvements in the attention of children from fourth to sixth grade. Findings showed they were less reactive and more able to handle daily challenges and choose their behaviour (Garey, 2023).

It is important to recognise how parents, early years staff and carers have a significant influence on children's early brain development and the time children spend playing, socially interacting and building on their interests supports their future outcomes and emotional wellbeing. With ongoing studies conducted around the world where mindfulness practices for young children are implemented, results have shown that the children who practiced mindfulness benefited with 'lowered aggression, social anxiety, and stress levels' as well as executive function, working memory and cognitive development (Azarian, 2016).

This shows how mindfulness enables children to build self-regulation skills and navigate uncertain times. Therefore, encouraging the participation of all staff in implementing daily mindfulness within the early years setting will greatly enhance staff wellbeing. It will also potentially benefit every child by incorporating simple activities such as sitting still and noticing the breath, walking, eating mindfully and talking about their feelings. When practicing mindfulness, even for a few minutes each day, children can learn to manage daily stressors and find ways to manage their emotions and return to a state of calm and improve both their physical and mental health. The government continue to provide information and guidance to support wellbeing for individuals and groups.

Case Study: Yasmin Mukadam, Researcher and University Lecturer

As senior lecturer at a university, I conducted an exploratory study to evaluate the impact of a mindfulness training programme for teachers in one school.

The aim of the research was to investigate if Mindfulness-Based Stress Reduction (MBSR) training can improve teachers' sense of wellbeing and enhance their professional practice.

Objectives of the research were to:

■ Evaluate a bespoke 19-hour MBSR programme for a group of teachers at one school

■ Explore if the training provides teachers with a set of tools and skills to develop self-efficacy and generate new ideas in classroom teaching

■ Identify other effects of introducing mindfulness into a school, flowing on from the reduction of teacher stress

MBSR training has been increasingly reported to have positive effects on mental health such as decreasing stress levels, in addition to increasing focus, attention and executive function. There is increased interest in mindfulness for teachers with Education professionals exploring the benefits and outcomes of what it takes to become a 'mindful' teacher.

A mixed measures approach was applied with four measures of assessment: Perceived Stress Scale, Philadelphia Mindfulness Scale, semi-structured interviews and reflective diaries. Data were collected at baseline and post-training with a sample of teachers from one independent school involved in the study ($N = 7$).

The results from the research suggested no significant difference in perceived stress level before and after the MBSR training. In the context of these findings, it needs to be emphasised that the school commended the participation of teachers' and their ability to accommodate the required add-itional hours to undertake the MBSR training. Teachers did report a significant increase in levels of wellbeing and reduction in stress levels according to the analysis of qualitative data.

Common benefits from the research included:

- A shared learning experience for participants

- Acknowledgement of present moment awareness

- Approaches supported stress reduction

- Identifying stressors within professional role

- Mindfulness incorporated into teaching and for own personal development

> My stress levels are lower and my capacity is growing. I am more com-passionate and kinder to myself.
>
> (Participant from research)

Research Findings: The study demonstrated that teachers benefit from a mindfulness training intervention. Mindfulness holds a mediating effect on teachers' level of wellbeing, both personally and professionally. The adapted course structure was more feasible for teachers, and this resulted in the positive results and high attendance at the training. Planned strategies to embed mind-fulness approaches within the school were recommended, for both teachers and children with consideration of a 'wellbeing instrument' for teachers and the development of a 'wellbeing centre' at the school.

Contact Yasmin Mukadam for further information.

Conclusion

A key theme throughout this book has been the developing relationship and engage-ment of mindfulness between the adults working with the children, the environment and the early years curriculum. With the continuing rising levels of mental health issues in young children, it is more important than ever to develop the social and emotional environment through practices such as mindfulness to support early intervention in children's lives, in order to positively impact on their future and bring about the ability to experiences calmness, relaxation, self-regulation skills and awareness. This supports the National Health Services (NHS) guidance that being 'mindful' is one of the five steps to a healthier mental wellbeing (Sellgren, 2016).

EYPs have a responsibility that extends beyond supporting the building blocks to formal education of children. This is to recognise the importance of developing the emotional and social development of children and build confidence so that children can self-regulate and learn skills to make decisions and rationalise the world and their place in it, maximising their learning opportunities. As children's brain develops, they are able to improve their attention, concentration and focus. This, in turn, enables them to think and plan their actions, known as executive function. Alongside this, the skill of self-regulation is vital for children's lifelong mental health and wellbeing, which Grenier (2021) reminds us and also emphasises how the revised Development EYFS includes self-regulation as a stand–alone early learning goal. As professionals working in the early years sector, it is everyone's role to provide a broad and balanced curriculum with opportunities, activities and experiences that enable children to manage and express their emotions and feelings and to become confident learners in all areas of their development (Mukadam and Sutherland, 2018).

The following are useful resources and information for early years settings:

Materials and resources for early years settings	Source
The Foundation Years resources for wellbeing and mental health	https://foundationyears.org.uk/2020/12/putting-wellbeing-at-the-heart-of-our-early-years-practice/
British Mindfulness Institute courses	https://www.britishmindfulnessinstitute.co.uk/
Government guidance about wellbeing	https://www.gov.uk/guidance/wellbeing
BBC Children in Need Mindfulness Hub	https://www.bbcchildreninneed.co.uk/schools/primary-school/mindfulness-hub/
Anna Freud Centre – Early years staff wellbeing: a resource for managers and teams	https://www.annafreud.org/media/14127/early-years-staff-wellbeing-resource-130721.pdf
Five strong benefits of workplace wellbeing	https://www.perkbox.com/uk/platform/perks/the-what-why-and-how-of-workplace-wellbeing
Early years foundation stage (EYFS) statutory framework	https://www.gov.uk/government/publications/early-years-foundation-stage-framework--2

(Continued)

Materials and resources for early years settings	Source
The Mental Health at Work Commitment	https://www.mentalhealthatwork.org.uk/commitment/
NHS Report – Mental Health of Children and Young People in 2020	https://files.digital.nhs.uk/AF/AECD6B/mhcyp_2020_rep
Mindfulness in Schools Project – dots curriculum (ages 3–6)	https://mindfulnessinschools.org/teach-dots-3-6/dots-curriculum-ages-3-6/
Mollie Wright: How every child can thrive by five| TED	https://youtu.be/aISXCw0Pi94
First Things First – Early Childhood Brain Development	https://www.firstthingsfirst.org/early-childhood-matters/brain-development/
Early Years Toolkit Promoting Wellbeing	https://www.oxfordshire.gov.uk/business/information-providers/childrens-services-providers/support-early-years-providers/early-years-toolkit/promoting-wellbeing
The Calm App	https://www.calm.com

References

Album, J. (2021) Early years staff say it's time to make staff wellbeing a policy. Accessed on 6 June 2022 at https://www.annafreud.org/insights/news/2021/07/early-years-staff-say-it-s-time-to-make-staff-wellbeing-a-policy/

Chartered Institute of Personnel and Development (CIPD) (2021), *Wellbeing at Work*. Accessed on 17 July 2022 at https://www.cipd.co.uk/knowledge/culture/well-being/factsheet#gref

Cherry, K. (2020) *What is Meditation?* Accessed on 2 February 2022 at https://www.verywellmind.com/what-is-meditation-2795927

Collard, P. (2014) *The Little Book of Mindfulness: 10 Minutes a Day to Less Stress, More Peace*. London: Octopus Publishing Group.

Department of Health (2014) What works to improve wellbeing. Accessed on 27 May 2022 at https://assets.publishing.service.gov.uk/government/uploads/system/uploads/attachment_data/file/277593/What_works_to_improve_wellbeing.pdf

Douglas-Osborn, E. et al. (2021) Anna Freud National Centre for Children and Families. Early Years Staff Wellbeing: A Resource for Managers and Teams. Accessed on 20 September 2022 at https://www.annafreud.org/media/14127/early-years-staff-wellbeing-resource-130721.pdf

Garey, J. (2023) *The Power of Mindfulness*. Accessed on 4 December 2022 at https://childmind.org/article/the-power-of-mindfulness/

Genier, J. (2021) The EYFS reforms: Priorities, opportunities and myths. Accessed on 9 June 2022 at https://www.headteacher-update.com/best-practice-article/the-eyfs-reforms-priorities-opportunities-and-myths-development-matters-birth-to-five-matters-dr-julian-grenier-reception-communication-skills/236813/

Heads Together for ABI Report (2019/20) Accessed on 14 April 2022 at https://headstogether. org.au/wp-content/uploads/2020/10/Heads-Together-Annual-Report-2019.20-compressed.pdf

Kinsner et al. (2018) *How Can Mindfulness Support Parenting and Caregiving, Literature Review.* Accessed on 30 June 2022 at https://socacrosstn.org/wp-content/uploads/2018/09/How-Can-Mindfulness-Support-Parenting-and-Caregiving_-A-Literature-Review.pdf

Mental Health Foundation (2021) *What is Mindfulness.* Accessed on 10 May 2022 at https://www.mentalhealth.org.uk/explore-mental-health/a-z-topics/mindfulness

Mind (2019) *Heads Together 'Mental Health for Small Workplaces' Online Training.* Accessed on 12 July 2022 at https://www.mind.org.uk/media-a/5795/mind-evaluation-of-htmhsw-online-training-final-report-v20.pdf

Mindfulness All Party Group (MAPPG) (2015) *Mindful Nation UK Report.* Accessed on 9 November 2022 at https://www.themindfulnessinitiative.org/mindful-nation-report

Mukadam, Y. and Sutherland, H. (2018) *Supporting Toddlers' Wellbeing in Early Years.* London: Jessica Kingsley Publishers.

Preschool Learning Alliance Report (2018) *Minds Matter, The Impact of Working in the Early Years Sector on Practitioners' Mental Health and Wellbeing.* Accessed on 29 October 2022 at https://www.eyalliance.org.uk/sites/default/files/minds_matter_report_pre-school_learning_alliance.pdf

Sellgren (2016) *National Health Service (NHS) 5 Steps to Mental Wellbeing.* Accessed on 23 October 2022 at https://www.nhs.uk/mental-health/self-help/guides-tools-and-activities/five-steps-to-mental-wellbeing/

World Happiness Report (2019) Accessed on 15 May 2022 at https://worldhappiness.report/ed/2019/

Index

Note: Page numbers in *italics* indicate figures and **bold** indicate tables in the text